# News for the Ear
## a homage to Roy Fisher

*– A Stride Conversation Piece –*

Other Stride books by Robert Sheppard:

*Far Language: poetics and linguistically innovative poetry 1978-1997*

*Empty Diaries*

*Daylight Robbery*

*The Flashlight Sonata*

*My Kind of Angel: i.m. William Burroughs*
[contributor]

*At The Heart Of Things: the poetry and prose of David Miller*
[contributor]

Other Stride titles available include:

*Binary Myths: conversations with contemporary poets*
edited by Andy Brown

*Binary Myths 2: correspondences with poet-editors*
edited by Andy Brown

*A State Of Independence* edited by Tony Frazer

*The ABCs of Robert Lax*
edited by David Miller and Nicholas Zurbrugg

*A Curious Architecture: a selection of contemporary prose-poems*
edited by Rupert Loydell and David Miller

*How The Net Is Gripped: a selection of contemporary American poetry*
edited by Rupert Loydell and David Miller

*A Gallery To Play To: the story of the Mersey Poets*
Phil Bowen

# News for the Ear
## a homage to Roy Fisher

*edited by*
Peter Robinson & Robert Sheppard

NEWS FOR THE EAR
First edition 2000
© Stride 2000
*All rights reserved*

Selection © the editors

Copyright of individual pieces
© individual authors

ISBN 1 900152 67 3

Cover art by Ronald King
Cover design by Neil Annat

*Published by*
Stride Publications
11 Sylvan Road, Exeter
Devon EX4 6EW
England

## Contents

*Invitation*  Peter Robinson & Robert Sheppard  7
*Gifts*  Edwin Morgan  8
*The Time, Saturday*  Roy Fisher  9
*At the Grave of Asa Benveniste*  Roy Fisher  12
*Item*  Roy Fisher  14
*Last Poems*  Roy Fisher  17
*License my Roving Hands*  Roy Fisher  18
*The Following Story*  Thom Gunn  45
*Left Hands and Wittgensteins*  John Matthias  46
*An Unpublished Commentary from 1966*  Gael Turnbull  47
*Hymn*  Tony Baker  50
*Admiring Mr. Fisher's Patent Cabinet*  Lee Harwood  51
from *City Walking (1)*  Jeremy Hooker  56
*Multiscreen*  Richard Caddel  58
*A Dirty Poem and a Clean Poem*  Robert Sheppard  60
*Travels with Roy*  Fleur Adcock  62
*The Thing About*  Maurice Scully  65
*In a Tight Corner*  Peter Robinson  66
*City Lights*  Elaine Feinstein  69
*Passing Harecops*  Peter Riley  70
*Get Real*  Ken Edwards  72
*Seven Variations…*  Maurice Scully  76
*The Poetry of Roy Fisher*  August Kleinzhaler  77
*Lament*  Sean O'Brien  78
*The Power of Magic*  Jeremy Hooker  80
*Bristol Night Walk*  Charles Tomlinson  83
*Freedom Forms*  Robert Sheppard  84
*Do Not Be Deterred*  Gael Turnbull  86
from *Futures*  Ken Edwards  87
*The Slink*  Peter Riley  89
*Dear Mr Fisher*  Carol Ann Duffy  91
*The Colors of the Days*  John Tranter  92
*Playing Dead*  Peter Robinson  94
*The Sky's Events*  Peter Robinson  95
*'Come to Think of It, the Imagination':*
Roy Fisher in Conversation with John Kerrigan  96
*Notes on Contributors  122*

## *Invitation*

Despite all evidence to the contrary, at some recessed level we perhaps still cling to the ancient belief that even our unwilling heroes are immortal. So the news, a few years back, that Roy Fisher had suffered a serious stroke came as a painful shock; and yet here he is, boldly undeterred, a wry and vigorous seventy. There need be no excuse of time on the clock to pay tribute to the author of *City, The Ship's Orchestra*, 'Matrix', 'Handsworth Liberties', 'Wonders of Obligation' and *A Furnace* – but there is a danger that, thinking our heroes immortal, we take their continued existence for granted. This is precisely what *News for the Ear: a homage to Roy Fisher* intends not to do.

Rather than fraternally signing manifestoes with like-minded peers or cultivating a lineage of disciples, Roy Fisher, without seeking any such thing, has accumulated an internationally broad range of advocates from the contemporary literary scene. As one of his possibly real correspondents in 'Paraphrases' confessed, 'I have articles by Davie, D., / and Mottram E.' – two impassioned poet-critics who once seemed to form the paired opposite limits of Fisher's consituency. The recent deaths of both these writers prevented us from inviting them to contribute to our homage, but we have concentrated on their like: the most passionately and intellectually involved of Fisher's admirers, the poets and writers themselves. We invited them to suggest, in prose, some aspect or feature of their admiration and to offer a poetic text, as a gift, to the birthday celebration. Some did one or the other; some felt able to do both.

A little later, it became clear that the requirements of the *Stride Conversation Piece* series would oblige us to abandon the idea of a surprise present for the poet, for we needed to ask him to contribute some uncollected work and to undertake a fresh interview. Despite his long-standing reluctance to rush into print, we were able to convince him to let us gather up some of his recent poems and a delightful series of radio talks broadcast over a decade ago. We were also lucky to be able to persuade John Kerrigan to turn some of his informal e-mail correspondence with Roy Fisher into a fully-fledged interview.

The result is a birthday party at which, as is only right, the guest of honour takes centre stage, after a toast by his senior poet friend Edwin Morgan. There follow the tributes from his various allies, and, finally, the interview in which as is again only right, Roy Fisher gets the last word. Writing in the *Poetry Review* some years ago, Elaine Feinstein observed that Roy Fisher's 'historical position seems assured' and with it, we believe, his literary immortality.

*Peter Robinson & Robert Sheppard*

## *Gifts*

The tarmac said: It's all right, wheel. Purr or roar,
 grit or gravel, smooth as steel or rough as rubble,
 bring miles, smiles, milestones, sandstone, stonechats,
 cats's eyes, cat-ice, chatoyant oil-pool pot-holes,
 all the spins and all the spit and spearmint and all
 the stains, all the ditches, all the drains, bring them
 oil and air and all, all the trains, all the rains,
 all the terrain, it's all ruts, it's all roots, it's
 all right. Bring.

The streetlamp said: Get it, collect it, fetch it, light
 slant and low or light flaring, fetch light, dull blue
 where the door-flung dynamo broods, petrol-blue on
 blear puddles, icy glimmer in the refrigeration van,
 get some red, steal the cigarette-glow from evening
 avenues, foggy signals at the viaduct, take it, take them,
 they are jewels. Add the high bright, the star, the wink,
 the planet, add Venus. Let the load stream to the party.

The whistle said: Gather the drum-rolls, roll up the riffs,
 hatful of hooters, splice the sirens with gulls and
 saxes, make a parcel, pack in parker parry parsifal,
 get a blast at last, pass the hat. And hang up that heat
 of the hoot, on the hook. Park your parting. Play in
 array. Sets for all clay.

The door said: Bang. It's a birthday.

*Edwin Morgan*

## *The Time, Saturday*

(1)

After years of sour flatus,
mind-lunges, sudden but dwindling
rages, he swells

when his knob-nose and
his stomach tell him he's
finally where it's to be had,

into his recrudescence. Having
no use for proportion,
structure, space,

he finds his genius lodges
in a place thick with himself.
A one-end street, a steep

wall-headed pitch with rubble, where tarmac
gives out and the scattered bricks
breed. Terraces worn,

filled with faces. Saturday sunset,
smoky. An old Buick
taxi, *Pride of the North*,

charging up the ruts. Hangs in, idles
like a cement-mixer, goes dead. Not all the people
assembled to witness the recrudesence

are drunk. Some have a permanent intentness.
One woman only totters, another
keeps herself crouched. Recriminations

go slanting off. Not all the speeches
get spoken, or could be. He's well-
buried into brick-ends, oilcans, glints of declining

sun on tea-set gilding; dust and sand
rubbed ruddy into his skin.
In him a god of opaque

grandeur lays claim on spirit, breathing
through gnawed-down hard-bake Roman brick
mortared with puke. Almost there comes

the clamping-on of cracked, rust-stained
marble cladding, the brandish
of a torn-out privet bush.


(2)

An hour into the cool and the dusk
with a move to a nearby
hall, and it's fading: the air

already too thin for anything
but ordinary breathing, and a group
standing statue around him at haphazard

angles under headroom. Among them
a caretaker, calling
music back down from the rafters.


(3)

Things falling flat. Everybody
who's left and can bend
gets into a drawer, folds down.

Off-centre under the low ceiling.
Strip-lights with shades come on. Talk
slopes back up, back down.


(4)

Well after midnight the set
still rubble, barely heaves, its cleaned-off
cubicles lit by numerous

low-flying moons that negotiate
passageways, manoeuvre through windows.
In a tidy corner, a room suddenly

filled with one, a great roofless
shout: 'GAO!' – one of the most
secret names of God. The lights

suddenly drain away upwards.
Near by, another voice: 'Got to get
some of these wet moons seen to...'

*Roy Fisher*

## *At the Grave of Asa Benveniste*

>                with Fleur Adcock and for Agneta Falk

Churchyard woman coming quickly from under the wall:
*You're looking for Plath.* No question-mark.

No short way out of it but
follow the finger, stand for a spell in the standing-place,

be seen, then duck off sidelong
to where under your stone
you're remarked on less:

Asa, translucent Jew,
your eyebrows arched
so high as to hold
nothing excluded that might want in,

it's proper to come your way,
by deflection. Exquisite poet,
exquisite – will the language say this? –

publisher; not paid-up for a burial
with the Jews, nor wanting
to have your bones burned,
ground up and thrown, you're here

in the churchyard annexe,
somebody's hilltop field walled round, a place
like the vegetable garden of an old asylum,

lowered from the drizzle in the hour between
service and wake, inventions that made life
stand up on edge and shake. The church

cleared for the People Show's
deepest dignities, *Kaddish*
by Bernard Stone, alternate
cries striking the nave in brass —

Nuttall from the floor, from the rafters
Miles Davis. Your house filled fast with stricken
friends muttering mischiefs up the stair

to the room where latterly
you'd lived mostly with the windows,

looking out, letting in, surrounded
by what used to be the bookshop stock,
priced up safe against buyers: *I can't have
anyone taking my good friends away from me.*

Afloat on the mood all day, Judi,
doing your looking-out for you
for a spell. From the middle of the room
to the window and through it, steadily
up towards Bell House Moor. Downstairs,

barrelhouse music and booze. On. Everybody.
Freed to be with you in your house again, the clocks
seriously unhitched. And visible in the crush
through the dark afternoon, Ken Smith, suit
worn at a rakish angle, the face worn
lightly if at all. And on we go.

The stone's as you asked for it:

FOOLISH ENOUGH TO HAVE BEEN A POET.

                              Asa,
your hat's in the bathroom.

                    *Roy Fisher*

## *Item*

A bookend.  Consider it well
if that's the way your mind
runs.  One-handed

this year at least, and lame,
unable to shift it somewhere better
than where it unbalances

one of the unsafe heaps that
make up my workroom, even I
get driven to consider it,

putting myself at risk of unaccustomed
irony, metaphor, moral.
It's one of a couple. The other's long-

lost in the house and has turned to pure
thought.  This one's material,
cut from three-quarter-inch softwood,

deep-stained as oak and varnished
heavily; a few scratches. Made up
of three pieces. The face,

five inches across by four-and-three-quarters,
with the corners cut in at forty-five
degrees from three inches up; two

nails struck through to the base,
same shape, but three by three-and-a-half,
hollowed and plugged with lead. A buttress

braces the joint. The outward
edges all bevelled, and the whole
glued solid. It's professional,

effective as a brick would be
but with less style. No trace
of commercial fancy anywhere on it.

When my life's props come to suffer dispersal
this piece gets dumped, if I've not
done it myself first. Should it get to a junk-stall

there'd be nothing to know but these
its observable properties. All the same
it does have unshakeable provenance - unless I

choose to suppress it. I don't.
I've certain knowledge the thing is fifty-two
years old, manufactured in 1944

at the enormous works of the Birmingham
Railway Carriage and Wagon Company,
the neighbourhood's mother-ship and provider,

her main East entrance
sunk in the bend of the street I lived in.
Set up to build saloons for the world's

railways. Then Churchill tanks. Then latterly
by day and night, huge helpless plywood-skinned
troop-carrier gliders that were crawled out

wingless and blind between the houses,
lacking engines, armour or arms. Lacking
bookends. The bookend maker was a foreman

coachbuilder from the top of the street,
a man of some status, genial; Mikhail
Gorbachev would be good casting if unemployed

when this poem's filmed. My bookends
formed part of a short, non-commercial,
privately-produced domestic series

using materials, tools and time stolen
from the Ministry of Aircraft Production
and its contract, and designed as family gifts

for the Friday firewatch team, four veterans
of the Great War who gathered as ordered
by law and played cards in an empty house all night,

never looking outdoors. Against
regulations, but less culpable
than the woodworking: it was forbidden

ever to reveal the sources of one's secret bookends.
The same foreman had an only daughter.
Well-provided: plenty of body, a job

in the factory office, a husband stationed
not far away, a home with her parents. Tapping
into a quiet custom of the time,

she worked out the date of her army call-up,
got pregnant, got herself certified so. Aborted
the foetus at home while the débris

was still small enough for the closet in the yard
to flush it; kept quiet, played for time;
won. Another little knot of illegalities.

As to this bookend, to say that the first
load it supported was a crimson-backed set of miniature
home encyclopaedias, forced into the house

in the newspaper wars of the Thirties by the agents
of Beaverbrook, later Minister of Aircraft Production
would be artistic, ironic, and, just possibly, untrue.

*Roy Fisher*

## Last Poems

Thinning of the light
and the language meagre;
an impatient shift under the lines

maybe to catch the way
the lens, cold
unstable tear, flattens and tilts
to show codes of what may be flaring
at the edge and beyond.

Absence of self-pity suggests
absorption in something or other
new, never to be defined.

But in all those years before
what *was* his subject?

*Roy Fisher*

## License my Roving Hands

I've played jazz on pianos, or the defunct, sodden carcasses of pianos, in hundreds of different establishments since the middle 1940s. But what to call those places? Jazz clubs? Sounds like somewhere specially built, like cocoa rooms or abattoirs; not true. Night clubs? Rarely, and on sufferance. Dance halls? Sometimes. Restaurants? Once in a while. I ought, I sometimes think, to have been pumping out this American-born music all these years in a succession of underground dens, cellars, furnished holes in the sidewalk. *Dives*. But hardly any of them have been that sort of place. Most of them have been up several flights of stairs, and very English indeed. For the overwhelming majority of these venues have been the more-or-less disused Function Rooms of old pubs, with buffalo horns, and bedroomy wallpaper above the brown panelling,

There's a further oddity. In all those years, I can only call to mind a handful of occasions on which I've entered one of those long, dark, linoleum-floored rooms for any purpose other than that of playing or hearing jazz. A small farewell supper for a local headmaster in a Devon market town; a brief sandwich lunch in Cromford, Derbyshire, for our educational coach tour of D. H. Lawrence country; and a couple of working meetings of the Birmingham and district project group of Centre 42. Now those were, as they say, something else. I was there as a jazz musician, but not to play; things hadn't got as far as that. For me they never did.

Arnold Wesker's Centre 42 movement of the early Sixties still has, for me, such a feeling of unfinished business, of unresolved issues, that I find it hard to realise that it all happened, or didn't happen, so long ago that it's bound to need explaining. It was a movement which aimed at raising Trade Union consciousness, and Trade Union funds, in the cause of discovering and fostering real, non-commercial popular culture: art by and for the people. The assumption was that the populace at large had its own arts locked up within it, and, more interestingly, *needed* those arts, and for more vital purposes than mere entertainment; it needed its own arts in order to live as a civilisation, instead of as nothing more than somebody else's army of workers and consumers – for it still seemed fairly natural then, as it would not seem so nowadays, to describe the majority of the population in terms of its work, and even of its membership of unions.

It all sounds uncommonly like – Socialism? Well, yes. That was the idea. A very old idea, of course; a noble old flagwaver of an idea, going back far beyond William Morris and Walt Whitman, and here surfacing once again, however much it had become muddied along the way by new sophistications. Indeed, my own first thought, when the summons to show interest came round in the Musicians' Union newssheet, was that this was all exactly like things I'd read about in accounts of the Left Wing arts movements of the Thirties – Unity Theatre, groups set up by the WPA in America, that sort of thing. But I decided all the same to turn out and see what might be going on. I couldn't imagine that this enterprise wasn't something completely fresh: even if you left the war out of account, and the great tidal movements of national and world politics, there had already occurred the first wave of the Campaign for Nuclear Disarmament, the first wave of Rock music and the first wave of mass television ownership; there had been invasions by foreign films and by the ideas of the Beat Generation; folk clubs were on the up; and there had even been a few changes wrought by bebop and the traditional jazz revival. And for those who live in worlds capable of being changed by such things, the world was about to be changed and out of all recognition and for ever by the Beatles and Christine Keeler. So I made my way one evening across yet another pub foyer floored with Victorian mosaic tiles, and up yet another brown staircase, to an upper room, with heavy tables, dark bentwood chairs, and tall windows that overlooked the back of New Street Station.

The gathering wasn't large, nor was it particularly heterogeneous, either; there may have been other stray members of various unions as well as me; I'm not sure. Whatever the details, however, the general makeup of the meeting soon became clear; for it was something I'd seen before, and which I've certainly seen many times since. We were a group of people mostly in what were still in those days thought to be safe middle-class occupations: teachers; an extremely distinguished BBC producer; a hefty presence of Communist Party members from the Public Library Service, the Council House, and also possibly from one or two departments of the University with a long history of that allegiance. And as for me, I was teaching in a College of Education, where the teachers had to be called *lecturers* – a title which had little relation to what most of us actually did, but which seemed to endow the job with an extra coating of protection from misfortune or squalor, even if didn't enhance our wretched pay.

At a guess, most of the people in the room were in publicly-funded, and probably pensionable, jobs. An old story. But there we were: wherever we'd started out from, individually, we'd got ourselves shunted, by way of education (mostly free), occupational aptitude, and taste, into a sort of siding of middle-class life, from which we were staring out across a social divide that separated us from a *lot* of people. Most people. I'm not suggesting that it was a total separation, or even a dramatic one; we weren't part of a wholly stratified society like that of the Eloi and the Morlocks in Wells's *The Time Machine* where two classes had lived in such separateness that they had eventually evolved into distinct species which might as well never have had a common origin. There were plenty of connections, but they were basic ones. Not all of the finer filaments of the cultural wiring managed to cross the gap, in either direction.

Some of us will have wished the divide had never come into existence; some of us, especially those who, like me, had been involuntarily airlifted across it in our sleep by the educational system, will have wished it had been less marked, so as to allow for free passage to and fro. There might just be a case for the odd Parish Boundary; there was certainly no warrant for the Berlin Wall. At all events, I suppose we were people who were unwilling to be stuck with only the higher forms of art as our only sustenance; and who, moreover, weren't simply in the business of carrying higher culture to the lower orders – or London culture to what London still called 'the provinces'. We were much more interested in something we suspected might be persuaded to flow in the opposite direction. Our belief – or hope, at the very least – was that there existed, *out there*, or *down there*, valuable knowledge, urgent messages, ways of communicating, which hadn't survived a century or two of erosion and suppression, only to be drowned in recent waves of consumer-pap. We wanted to make contact.

But as soon as that meeting started to get down to a practical programme, I began to experience an inescapable sensation of being gradually squeezed out on to the periphery. And I was never for a moment in any doubt as to which of the people in the room was doing the squeezing: *I* was. There was something going on that wasn't going to work for me, and as the discussion went on I came to feel that I could neither beat it nor join it. This was in spite of the fact that I had – and still retain – a great respect for the work of our strongest asset: the radio producer. This was Charles Parker, a most talented and demanding man, one of the earliest virtuosi of the portable tape-recorder and a pioneer – if you can give that title to somebody whose work wasn't fully followed up – of a form of documentary radio art which worked by letting people speak entirely for themselves, having edited out all traces of the professional broadcaster and interviewer. All traces, that is except the unmissable trace of the hand of the director, who shapes the whole thing; I did say 'art'. Parker died at sixty, a few years ago, after a period of comparative inactivity and frustration; but at the time I'm speaking of he was in full flight, having quite recently produced, to considerable acclaim, the best examples of the genre he devised, the Radio Ballad. For the Centre 42 project, he was undertaking to oversee a sort of live Radio Ballad, a mixture of documentary material, dramatisation, songs and instrumental music. It was to be a touring show, which would play Labour Clubs, Miners' Institutes and the like, in various manufacturing centres around the Midlands.

It sounded good, and I believe it turned out so, though I never managed to catch it, when it eventually took the road. There was certainly plenty of talent and experience in the room that night; much of it from the folk-music revival end of things. I suppose that was an element in my self-imposed squeeze-out. Two things were clear: one, that music in the folk-song idiom, genuine or newly-minted, was integral to the production; two, that most of the people present had worked together before and had many assumptions, and a good deal of optimism, in common. I seemed to have dealt myself all the doubts. There wasn't, for instance, any real need for jazz in the production, though there was a willingness to make room for it as a tinge, a coloration, a particular form of expressive energy. The fact that there seemed to be no possible opening for what jazz players, on whatever instrument, sometimes just call *blowing* – letting fly, exercising their faculties at large – wasn't the fault of the project. Had there been other jazz musicians interested, we might have set up an additional project of our own, based on the music; but I was the only one, so I'd have to fit in where I could.

I did try fitting in; but as I listened to the planning, the doubts grew and grew, and they were ideological. Not in terms of straight politics, but in terms of what the potential audience was *like*. I seemed to feel a kind of missionary conviction in the air around me, and as the actual material of the production began to be roughed out, I could see that the Socialist Realism of the thing wasn't going to square with the day-to-day realism of anybody in the bit of the working class I'd come from. For a start, it was all about *work*. And it was going to develop – interestingly enough – into a sort of hymn to the technology of heavy industry. I could see the point of taking the technical wonders of the means of production and drawing them to the attention of those who used those wonderful means but certainly didn't own them; but going straight into the subject seemed to me like jumping the gun. I realised that in the minds of my potential colleagues that gun had been jumped long since. I *was* back in the Thirties after all.

Then came the real wave of doubt. The proposed title went through on the nod. It was 'The Worker and His Tool'. I couldn't believe what I was hearing. I looked furtively around. Not a grin, not a flicker anywhere. Titles for the sections were apportioned: they were things like 'The Shaping of the Tool'; 'The Hardening of the Tool'; 'The Fitting of the Tool'. Memory may exaggerate; but not by much. I didn't dare speak my thoughts. I could envisage the ring of heads turning frozen, uncomprehending stares on me. Who was this sniggering, insecure troublemaker, this slanderer of the seriousness of the worker? So I kept my doubts to myself; with the result that I impressed myself with them, if nobody else. Maybe these people really did know something I didn't? Maybe they'd lived among secret tribes of car workers and blast-furnace operators whose very existence had been hidden from me all my life? If I shut up and did my bit I might learn something new after all.

My bit turned out to be something I simply couldn't deliver, and that was why the second meeting was my last. My assignment had been merely to get hold of a couple more jazz instrumentalists, a double-bass player and a drummer, and get them interested in the project.   That has an air of bland possibility about it: why not? I'll tell you why not. Somehow I had to tell the working party why not, but I can't imagine they believed me. I was being asked to create economic havoc. The musicians I was after worked all day in factories, for money. Almost every night of the week they were out playing, for money – and bass players and drummers never came cheap, let alone free. Earning money may just have been a bad habit they'd got into; but I knew from the start that I had no chance of persuading any of them to forgo afternoons and evenings' wages in order to hare off to Atherstone or Wellingborough in pursuit of a cause. I couldn't deliver any bodies. A pity; but there it was.

At that second meeting, though, I wasn't the only spot of teething trouble. A Labour Club in one town couldn't accept the show on the night it could get there, on account of its unshakeable commitment to its own Bingo; in another town the Miners' Club bar, with its fruit machines and juke-box, could on no account be closed during the performance; a genuinely proletarian melodeon player who had been found in a village mostly given over now to executive housing had shown no interest whatever in joining a visit to the City gasworks to meet the workers there and share views. There was a certain impatience in evidence in the upper room that night; it was not far from the situation in that sarcastic poem of Bertolt Brecht's, where he suggests that the government might find things easier if it were to dissolve the people and elect another. It was time for me to fade away from the enterprise, baffled and still surprised at what I'd found; and go back down that particular set of stairs, with never a note struck in anger.

*

Anyone who gets, professionally or semi-professionally, into the business of assembling groups of musicians for dances, clubs or private functions, builds up a very important, and usually rather eccentric, book of telephone numbers. I'm talking only about jazz, or jazz-related music: the sort of thing that relies a good deal on improvisation and on a set of ideas about instrumentation and repertoire, which all the players who are likely to get booked will have in common. They don't even have to share a common language: I once – in Holland, as it happens – had to play a set of trombone-and-piano duets with an Argentinian trombonist. In spite of the fact that some of his musical colleagues had quite recently been sent out, against their wills, by Galtieri and killed, against my will, by British troops, our only problem of communication was finding an interpreter for the words, 'What are we going to play, then?' For it turned out that he knew the English for *Misty* and *Everybody Loves My Baby*, I knew the chords, so we were all set. For both of us, the musical challenge – maybe we met it, maybe we didn't – was the business of working out, as we went along, how to make a reasonable sound out of just a trombone part and just a piano part – a combination which probably neither of us had tried before. It's strange, but had we been put into a full seven-piece band made up of players from seven different countries we would have had a better idea of what to do.

The whole game, in fact, consists of having a reasonable idea in advance of where your particular instrument ought to fit into the general ensemble sound, and then being ready to modify that idea as quickly as possible to match the real sounds you hear around you when the band starts playing. And you do this *while* the band's playing. Rehearsals are very uncommon; partly because rehearsal fees are even more uncommon, but partly because lifelong buskers get to pride themselves on being able to live a bit dangerously and keep a straight face. I remember once waiting to go on as a member of a band which had been cobbled together to accompany the veteran American cornet-player, Wild Bill Davison. The entire preparation for the performance consisted of his turning and saying, semi-seriously, 'Now listen, let's get all the hellos over back here. No shaking hands with one another on the bandstand; that kinda thing can make the customers feel uneasy.' This brave man had never yet, I think, heard a note from any of us; I have to say that had he done so, *he* might have been feeling uneasy.

Classical musicians used to have a derogatory term: *a telephone orchestra*. Just the same sort of thing, but with a necessary added touch of bitterness. This would be an orchestra consisting of all too many substitutes, assembled by phone and often, in effect, providing the conductor of a concert with a quite different ensemble from the one he'd rehearsed – and whose absent members, incidentally, had been paid for the rehearsals. In the sort of music I'm talking about, though, the title wouldn't be derogatory; all the bands are telephone orchestras.

And that's where the books of phone numbers come in. I said they tended to be eccentric, and so they do. Mostly they're bottom-heavy. It's the bottom of the band, the drummers and bass-players, who rate the most entries. There'll be a fair number of trumpet-players and saxophonists, quite a few pianists, and even the odd trombonist or two; but there'll be page upon page of bassists and drummers. This isn't because there are more of them in existence. It's because you have to ring up more of them before you find one who's free, and willing to turn out. A lot of wheedling has to go on, and there's call for a variety of techniques. Depending on your nerve, you can either play safe, and book your rhythm team months ahead, when a freelance will accept almost any engagement in order to have something, at least, in an empty diary – the risk you take is that something better will turn up in the interim; or you can go for serious brinkmanship, and delay ringing round until teatime on the day of the gig, in the hope of taking one by surprise while feeding or at a moment when he's glad of a reason to be out of the house for the evening. That would happen only very rarely: bass-players work so many nights that their wives tend to be particularly tenacious of the nights they have at home. Or so they say.

If your brinkmanship should fail, you're in trouble, of course. Bands designed to have solid underpinning sound thin and helpless without it, so there's a practical reason for all this tyranny from below. I have to say that it's not as severe as it was a couple of decades ago, when the arrival of rock music and the bass guitar opened things up by increasing the supply of people who could play some sort of bass line. But before that it was a perennial burden, a negative, dissuasive element, like a state censorship or a currency-export limit. It was like a left-over wartime shortage.

In those days at least, bass players, and to a slightly lesser extent, drummers, had an image rather like that of the miller in a mediaeval village. They owned expensive, elaborate and essential items of technology; they knew their worth in market terms and drove hard bargains. They could lift you up, and they could let you down. And they never did anything for nothing. If a band was forming, or rehearsing new material, or preparing for a broadcast, the bassist and drummer would always flatly decline to rehearse, on the grounds that *they* didn't need to sweat over the parts like the brass and reed players, thank you very much; so long as the pianist was there to vamp the harmonies, that would do nicely. And they always had another job that night, in some dance band or other. In fact, they often had another job on the nights you thought they were booked with you; it would turn up at short notice, and be better paid. They'd send a dep – no need to rehearse him. No *point* in rehearsing him, either, in some instances.

For there were two types of bassist. There were bass-players, and there were bass-owners. The bass-owners formed a sizable, strange sub-class, which outnumbered the bass-players by about five to one. They were people who had bought a double-bass as an investment, and had learned just enough to make a generalised, fairly rhythmical, low humming or thudding noise on it. Not, you must understand, any actually identifiable notes. They could only get away with it on a low-register instrument. On a trumpet or a clarinet, they would have been rumbled at once, if not actually lynched by audiences; but down among the dead notes, they were on to a good thing. They sounded more or less like those home-made broomstick-and-tea-chest basses the Skiffle groups had in the Fifties, but they looked much more acceptably expensive; in fact some of the basses were really handsome instruments, and their owners often had looks to match. They were what you got on the night your bass-*player* suddenly got a better job. And your gig, in turn, was what they got in return for their investment. They were the millers *par excellence*. They got by without grinding much corn at all. Typical was One-Note-Jack, a tall, doleful man, who hardly moved, once he'd planted his bass and himself at the back of the stand, and was never known to pluck more than the first beat of a four-beat bar.

I talk about these people in the past tense, although there are still quite a few about – even One-Note-Jack, as I was surprised to learn only the other day. I suppose that in the thirty years since I last heard him he's only got through what would be seven-and-a-half-years' notes for a proper bassist, so he may still be feeling quite fresh. But the advent of bass-guitar players did undercut the investment structure somewhat, in that their instruments were rather cheaper to buy and easier to learn to play properly; so they found their way into the dance bands and even into some of the jazz groups, where their comparatively easy-going natures made up in part for the nastiness of the instrument they played. For some reason, too, they were easier to book than either the double-bass players or the double-bass owners. I suspect they're a different breed: failed guitarists, quite a few of them, and of a lighter temperament than men whose first impulse had been to go in low and strong. But they do share one characteristic with their colleagues who use what tends these days to be called the Upright Bass. They all lurk in their dens, waiting to be called on; they're very unlikely to provide work for others, in the way that trumpet players and saxophonists frequently do. And, with the towering and troubled exception of the late Charles Mingus, it's very rare for a good bass player actually to lead a band. Fisher's Fourth Rule of Engagement states that a bassist who offers employment is very unlikely indeed to be proficient, and that the financial incentives must be weighed very carefully against the potential suffering. A splendid example of the sort of man who owns both a bass and a band is the odious Sven Klang, in the film, 'Sven Klangs Kvintet'; his way of talking into the microphone while continuing to thud away gives all the warning anyone could need.

Mind you, I did have early leanings towards the lower register myself. At my school there was a concept called the School Orchestra, really a random collection of instruments which were periodically issued to keen boys. The idea was that each keen boy should take away his oboe, viola or French horn, somehow learn to play it, and come back ready to be directed into an ensemble by the Music Master. What *he* got out of this annually-repeated pretence I still can't imagine. I know I never heard a sound out of any of the school instruments. Had I been able to get my hands on one, I'd have made a noise on it all right; but I was only a fairly keen – or, more accurately, a fitfully keen – boy, and I was doubly thwarted by the militarism of the place and of the time. The instrument I wanted most of all was the clarinet, but my claim was topped by that of a smart boy who had a louder singing voice, and who was moreover an ornament of the School Air Training Squadron; I believe it was thought that, armed with his clarinet, he could in some way lead a mutation of the Cadets' extremely basic drum-and-bugle band into a full military band, of the sort that has silver saxophones and glockenspiels on sticks.

Plan B was the school double bass. I must have been going through a phase of having a rather mystical attitude to music, and to that instrument in particular; for a start, I couldn't find anybody who had ever seen it. I was an awestruck novice musician, and that meant that I didn't see learning to play as a matter of dexterity, perfectly-absorbed tuition and fidelity to a score; I approached it as a forest of forbidden sounds, never before heard, or even imagined. I thought of the double bass as the deepest repository of the darkest roots of sound. I didn't give a thought to the sheer effort of lugging it about, or building up my wrist muscles on the fingerboard. But where *was* the thing? It was a strongly Christian school, and enough of that had rubbed off to make me understand that you could have faith in the existence of something even if nobody could show it to you. So I believed in the school double bass, lying there among the foundations where it had been stowed at the start of the war four or five years earlier, as a precaution against bombs. Since when the Air Training Corps had built up over its hiding place a stack of their fireproof filing cabinets, secret records and armaments. There existed no protocol by which the stack could be breached. And as an only fitfully-keen boy, I lacked the stamina to lean on the Squadron on my own behalf.

Particularly since I was only a civilian, one of the effete set who elected to spend drill afternoons learning something called Civics from the woolly-mannered, ineffectual-looking Pacifist Master. I now know the Civics to have been a most incisively logical anarchism, and pretty good of its kind; as for the Pacifist Master, he was a Quaker historian, an Oxford don who appeared to have been sentenced to a spell of teaching in our school as a kind of penance, or as war work. If he was a Conscientious Objector, the authorities may well have slyly sent him to our school for the pleasure of seeing him sweating it out in a quasi-military establishment. He certainly did his bit for peace so far as my education went. I could tell he'd made his mark by the way some of the other masters ridiculed him in retrospect as soon as the shooting stopped and he went back to Oxford.

Anyway the school double bass, that musical Moby Dick, was never to surface in my time. Had I managed to get hold of it I might in time have managed to invest in a bass of my own. It could have turned into a nice little earner over the years. But I went home and struggled with our ageing piano. It had playable notes for a couple of octaves above Middle C, but for nearly three octaves going downwards; and I'm left-handed anyway, so I could set myself up for a few years of mysterious growling and banging down there. I was victimised in the end, though: I fell into the clutches of a calculating bandleader who realised I could be tricked into doing the bass-player's job with my left hand as well as my own with my right, all for one man's pay. So he sacked the bass-player. Then I quit. Then he persuaded the guitarist to add the piano chords and the bass line to his own part. He had to contort himself dreadfully in order to do it, of course. I haven't heard of that guitarist for a long time. The bandleader's comfortably off.

*

When I was about eighteen, and something of a veteran in the business of daring to bang out a small repertoire of ill-fingered tunes at jazz sessions around Birmingham, I started to form the idea of early retirement; and before I was twenty, I'd done it. For the first time, anyway. I couldn't imagine that I wasn't soon going to grow out of it. I didn't know I was hooked on this music, and was already part of a network which was spreading quietly and rapidly, particularly at that time, the late Forties: a network made out of something strong, and so extensive that fresh bits of it are still coming into view, even now.

You can see evidences of it in what I think of as a benignly pathological jazz-addiction, or provocative, incantatory *naming* of jazz in places where it can't be guaranteed to produce goodwill, though it might. The playwright Alan Plater's a good example of somebody who uses his media-access to wave a jazz flag. The plot of the television series *The Beiderbecke Affair*, which could have started anywhere Plater chose, starts with an order placed by the amiable hero, Trevor Chaplin, for a set of tapes of recordings made by Bix Beiderbecke in the late Twenties. As a character, Trevor Chaplin is a sort of open space – an allotment, perhaps – rather untidily planted with a collection of Alan Plater virtues: innocence; suspicion; feeling; resistance to humbug; general Northerliness; a wary commitment to women; complete commitment to football; complete commitment to jazz. Now the football, for the purposes of run-of-the-mill television drama, would have done on its own; but it's played down in favour of the jazz, which gives the character a touch of irrationality the drama needs. I guess pathological addiction to football on its own wouldn't be thought irrational at all.

But Trevor Chaplin's jazz-addiction isn't the pin-headed, nit-picking specialism which could be offered as the jazz-collector's equivalent of blind loyalty to the home team. For him, the home team is practically the whole of jazz music, from King Oliver to Sonny Rollins, Miles Davis and Toshiko Akiyoshi and Lew Tabackin – all those names he rolls off his tongue as he rummages through the records in Big Al's warehouse. They're all emblazoned on the banner. It's not Swing against Bop, or Blues against Big Bands; it's Jazz in General against Creeping Evil. And it is, as I said, an incantation, a naming of names: not much actual jazz was played in *The Beiderbecke Affair* for all the allusions to jazz in the jolly soundtrack. But the name Beiderbecke is, as anyone familiar with the history and hagiography of jazz knows, no ordinary word. It's a magical one, which works in much the way the name 'Gatsby' has come to do, suggesting far more than it denotes.

I picked on *The Beiderbecke Affair* because it's a particularly meritorious example of the injection of a jazz loyalty which is, strictly speaking, somewhat surplus to the requirements of its surroundings. But you can spot others, once you know what you're looking for. There is in Bill Cosby a team loyalty to the work of black jazz musicians which goes a little beyond his general programme of systematically subverting all the old images of black people – whether as devils incarnate or Uncle Tom – by sanitising them into the world of a Middle-American sitcom. He plugs the acknowledged heroes of black achievement, like Count Basie, or Ray Charles, but there's a little extra warmth, a touch of the adolescent with a grown-up cheque book, about the way he makes sure it all gets in the script. And there's the curious matter of Cliff Huxtable's old father. This character is a tame and folksy old fellow, who looks as if he'd be an Uncle Tom if only there were any white folks for him to suck up to; but Cosby makes him a retired jazz trombonist, putting his feet up and dedicating himself to orgies of family piety after what seems to have been a career in a band of really hard men – something like one of the early editions of Art Blakey's Jazz Messengers. I can't imagine Art Blakey himself getting like that; but never mind. The jazz fan in Cosby gets his foot in the door.

They're always doing it. John Wain wrote a jazz novel and some jazz poetry; and although their writings about it occupy separate compartments, away from their poetry and fiction for the most part the way in which jazz fed Philip Larkin and Kingsley Amis from boyhood on is plain to see. The historian Eric Hobsbawm borrowed the name of the black trumpeter Frankie Newton for his critical writings on jazz. And I remember how the novelist Jack Trevor Storey angled to get the American saxophonist and personage Bud Freeman lined up for a part in his fantasy-autobiography on television, only to be foiled by employment regulations.

Then there are the persistent players, the incurable second line; the people whose main career has been in another art, or a profession in which their eminence might not seem consistent with the need to slope off and play in the local jazz club, or drive to distant cities by night, unable to resist a gig. Even without crossing the Atlantic to recruit Woody Allen, you can make the point with better clarinet players. There was the acoustic architect Sandy Brown; there's the cartoonist Wally Fawkes; there's the film critic Ian Christie; there's the artist Alan Cooper. Other names; Alan Davie, painter and avant-garde jazz cellist; Barry Fantoni; Jeff Nuttall; Russell Davies.

Apart from sharing that habit of perpetual truancy into music, I've also gone out of my way to earn a modest place in the complete file of case histories of unwarranted jazz naming. A boyhood hero of mine was the Chicagoan pianist Joe Sullivan. By the mid-Sixties he was an obscure and neglected figure and near the end of his life; his old records weren't getting reissued. While assembling poems for a collection I wrote one – I called it *The Thing*

*About Joe Sullivan* – which was really my version of what I'd have liked to read as the sleeve note of a new Joe Sullivan album, had there been one. It was about Joe Sullivan, and about my own abiding enthusiasm for his music. And I decided to make it the title poem of the book; not because it typified the whole collection, which it didn't, but because I thought it would be nice for me to see Joe Sullivan's name on the cover of a book. What with the ups and downs and ins and outs of publishing, the book when it finally appeared had a different form and had to have a different title; but I carefully kept that poem back, in case the chance came up again. And some ten years and three books later I remembered it and lifted it out of storage and on to a cover; so that the name of Joe Sullivan forced its way that year into the homes of some hundreds of members of the Poetry Book Society. And on the strength of that I somehow managed to get Granada Television to have the idea of letting me play in a group with Bud Freeman – who actually worked with Joe Sullivan – on a programme where I read my Joe Sullivan poem. So I was one up on Jack Trevor Storey for a few minutes.

All this, though, after retiring at twenty, convinced that a youthful canter was on its last legs. For it had been very much a peer-group activity of a particular late-teenage crowd, born between 1928 and 1930 and young enough to miss being called up while the war was still on. Almost without exception we were at, or just leaving, one of about five of the city's Grammar Schools; one or two went into National Service at eighteen, but most seemed to hang around for years on student deferments or with medical disabilities which didn't show themselves in civilian life.

We could tell we were a generation on our own just by the feel of things. It may have been different in all those other towns where, unknown to us at first, something of the kind was simultaneously going on; but the Birmingham crowd developed with a clear feeling of having no predecessors. We knew nobody at all older than ourselves who had ever tried to do what we were trying to do to rescue what was in fact a brief quarter-century of jazz history, not just by collecting records but by actually playing the stuff. In fact, most of us didn't know any older musicians at all. We behaved as if playing music had just been invented. We did know some older record collectors, just back from the war, and they were our first real audiences and our first promoters; but the actual musicians of that generation, who had spent the late Thirties and early Forties keeping up with the latest styles, were back in town making good money in dance bands, and, so far as the music went, disappearing fast into Bebop, where we couldn't have followed them even if we'd wanted to. We didn't even want to try Swing, let alone Bebop. In our crowd of young antiquarians I was regarded as quaintly modernistic, in that I was trying to copy styles popular from the late Twenties to the mid-Thirties, and was worrying my way dangerously towards the edge of the abyss, which was supposed to have opened up some time in 1936, after which everything was plunged into corruption: my purist friends planted their allegiances safely at the beginning of recorded time – acoustically recorded, that is, through enormous megaphone-like horns. But then, they weren't going in for half measures; and I was, strenuously. It's something to do with my character. I figured we had a good deal in common with the nicely brought-up young white boys from Chicago who had been bowled over in the Twenties by the black music from New Orleans, and I thought they should be our models; with more rigorous logic, my friends marched straight to the much more common conclusion, and tried very hard to believe they *were* black men from New Orleans.

Not that those older local musicians – they were mostly about twenty-five – were on speaking terms with any of us at that time. Later on, some of us learned to play just about well enough to keep up with them, as well as moderating our own archaic tastes; and a few of them gave way with advancing years to a little nostalgia for the records and the tunes of their youth, so we met halfway. But mostly they must, on the odd occasions when they heard us filling in as intermission bands, or on carnival floats, have been appalled and disgusted by our impassioned primitivism. By our turnout, too. With demob suits, know-how and a few fiddled clothing coupons, they could manage to look quite smart: loud check jackets with padded shoulders, dark trousers, light tan shoes, wide ties, shirts in interesting colours. Whereas we were reduced by need to what our ideology led us towards anyway, the dress of poor, off-duty cotton-pickers: open-necked white shirt, grey flannels, battered black shoes. The only leeway for personal style was in the size of your wristwatch, and whether you wore it facing outward or round on the inside of your wrist.

Really farouche was the brief vogue for wearing a straight-necked jersey *inside* the shirt, so that a triangle of it showed at the V, T-shirt fashion. Two snags to that. One was that wool was so hard to come by – a typical source was unpicking and dyeing wartime Balaclava helmets – that nobody's mother was ever going to knit a jersey other than the standard sleeveless V-neck, suitable for wearing with a collar and tie; the second was that wearing a jersey under your shirt tickles terribly. The first snag could be partially overcome: you wore your V-neck jersey back-to-front under your shirt. There was a snag to that of course: if you took off your Utility, non-fitted Harris-tweed-type jacket, the V of your jumper, plunging suggestively between your shoulder-blades, showed through your shirt. About the other snag, the tickling, there was nothing at all to be done. I suffered so much that I soon gave up the fancy. But my fellow-pianist Ray Foxley, who, if I remember rightly, introduced it, never seemed troubled – having in any case an eloquent Adam's apple, an expressively-raised chin and an unruffled faraway look. Besides, he was actually being the late Jelly-Roll Morton at the time. The piano-playing was already very like Morton's, and we were on the lookout for the arrival of the personal trademarks – the astrakhan-collared overcoat, the diamond rings, the diamond in the front tooth – even if they would have looked odd on the bus from Bromsgrove. I don't think Jelly-Roll Morton, even in his years of neglect, ever wore his jumper inside his shirt.

All in all, then, it seemed to be a matter of temporary lifestyle rather than the first stage of a career in music, professional or semi-professional, for any of us. We didn't fit either of those categories: we were amateurs, and no doubt about it. We played to try to match the noises in our heads, or our gramophones, and what anybody else made of it was *their* lookout. At first, they told us to stop; later, they'd tolerate us; much later, some of them would pay some of us – and that would take us over the line into the strange world of semi-professionalism, which simply means that you get paid for playing, but not often enough to make a living at it.

But around 1950, the original amateur gang was scattering and nothing seemed to be moving forward. Retirement seemed attractive. The young lady I was walking out with at the time – she played the viola – caught me listening to a Sidney Bechet record and said it was animal, the voice of depravity. Impressed, I retired there and then, and took up poetry which at least *looked* clean. Then she dropped out of my life – actually got a doctor's note; that was enterprising. But I stayed in retirement for a year or two. Then I started playing again, whenever I couldn't help it; and I've carried on ever since. And still, whenever I get access to one of the media, I slip in a plug for Joe Sullivan.

\*

My very first public performance as a pianist was also one of the rare occasions when I've been billed as a bandleader; I've quite often had my name attached to a trio, but that's just a result of the quaint convention by which pianists are supposed to be the leaders of rhythm sections. Anybody who thinks that should try it sometime. It's a misconception similar to the one which leads people – promoters and club managers more often than not – to come up and engage a band's pianist in conversation, on the grounds that, unlike the players with their eyes shut and things stuck in their mouths, he's not doing anything with his head. As the song doesn't have it, I'd rather *not* lead a band.

But here's how I came to be the leader of Roy Fisher and his Students of Jazz. The school I went to wasn't one of those with a strong jazz cell, enough people to form a six-piece band; my year had a trombonist and a banjo-player; there was a pianist a couple of years ahead of me, who gave it up to become a high-powered scientist; there was another pianist a couple of years behind me, and a drummer as well. Both became professors, but didn't give it up. In fact, they're still at it.

So: we were thin on the ground, and too many of us were pianists. But there was also Horseface. Nobody called him that, and it didn't have much relation to what he looked like; it was just a name he'd have liked to be called, instead of Leslie. This whim was the only illogicality about him, for Horseface was an extremely sensible boy; he got more done than most of us but strode through his adolescence with an awesome sense of his own limitations. He was a good artist, and trained as a painter, but wouldn't paint, for some sound reason or other; he was an excellent mechanic and knew all about cars, but certainly wouldn't be such a madman as to drive one; he was – how can I put it? – formidably celibate, in all directions, under the stern law of his sense of self-preservation. He also knew a great deal about jazz, and was a very enthusiastic and perceptive hand with a gramophone; and somewhere along the line he'd managed to become a very tidy trumpet-player. What he did with this accomplishment was odd, though; he spent his Saturday evenings, crammed into an ancient-looking dress suit, playing third trumpet in Jack

Bradney's Dance Orchestra in some Black Country Baths Ballroom or other. But he wouldn't venture on jazz – not on the instrument anyway; if you could have taken down his excitable conversation about Louis Armstrong or Roy Eldridge, and processed it through a trumpet, you'd have had jazz all right. It was as if he knew too much about it to want to do it for himself; the exact opposite of the standpoint of our amateur mob. The less we knew, the keener we were. And Horseface really belonged with us, and not with the Saturday-night semi-pros he earned his pocket-money with.

For a time, I thought his resistance was going to crack. In addition to working in the big band, he had also come by a regular engagement with a strange four-piece dance band. As well as himself, it consisted of a pale young commercial artist on clarinet and saxophone, who wanted to play jazz; a nice lady called Auntie Ivy Tonks, who was in fact the clarinet-player's aunt, on piano; and on drums, a breezy, rather old young man who was like something out of Surtees by way of the wartime RAF – as an update, you could add Basil Brush. He was quite well-to-do, but seemed to have a heavy hormone build-up, and liked to lay about himself and kick up a bit of a racket on his drum-kit; so *he* might be ready to fall into jazz, too. I rather think Auntie Ivy was out of all this, and probably kept getting better offers besides; at any rate, Horseface persuaded himself that I'd taught myself enough piano to help out with the band in her absence. This wasn't true. I was fifteen, and my total experience consisted of about a year of messing about with three chords in the keys of C and F. And I could think of no way in which I could explain to my parents that I was going to go out into the adult world after dark, dressed in a borrowed waiter's outfit; indeed, there was no way of raising the subject of my going out into that world at all. But one summer evening I did manage to slip away to join a practice with the three others.

It was the first time I'd ever heard a dance band, live, and the surroundings were extraordinary. The drummer was heir to a medium-sized factory, in a back street near the city centre, and the band rehearsed in the works canteen. I've forgotten what the factory produced, but the sensations of trailing through the deserted works, up and down rickety wooden stairs in the warm evening sunlight are still with me; and the thought of the particular degree of tunelessness of the canteen piano brings back the agreeably overpowering scent of sawdust and oil which filled the entire place. The other overpowering thing was the colossal din the drummer produced the moment he started to play. I could see his enormously cheery, handlebar-moustachioed face above the flailing cymbals, floating above this agony of noise, which was magnified and mangled by the bare walls of the canteen.

It didn't take me long to prove to the others that I wasn't yet ready to be exposed to people who knew a Veleta from a St. Bernard's Waltz, and that I probably never would be. But they wanted to make use of me for something. The first thing they did was to let me take part in a private recording session, at the drummer's expense. To record, even if you had to pay for it, was still a most romantic thing to do. The domestic tape recorder was still nearly ten years in the future, and there was nothing casual about it. You were recorded direct on to a single-sided soft acetate disc. Each tune cost a pound; each copy cost a pound. This was at a time when the 78s we collected cost five-and fourpence-halfpenny; so your own vanity, if you bought a copy of what you'd recorded, was pushing you into rating yourself at seven or eight times what you'd lay out on Duke Ellington or Art Tatum. Moreover, the records were so delicate that if you played them with an ordinary needle it would instantly plough the music off the disc in thin coils of black swarf, so you had to get expensive trailer needles; even so, the things wore out pretty quickly.

Our session was in what turned out to be a converted front bedroom over Mr. Jackman's radio shop in Birchfield Road, Lozells. I finished my homework early, and cycled down there, prepared to record six tunes. This was at least two more tunes than I knew; but I was willing to stretch a point. It was something of a relief for me to find a second pianist there – or, rather, to find that *I* was the second pianist. George, a very snazzy young player who did in fact go on to distinguish himself in the profession, but hadn't at that time got further than being one of Auntie Ivy's occasional deps, had just had his call-up papers, and the session had been hastily rededicated as a wake to George's youth. He knew all the tunes. But I was to be allowed to do two.

Mr Jackman's bedroom had a shiny black baby grand, and that fascinated me more than the recording equipment; I'd never been allowed to get my hands on anything like that before. George, with sleek American hair – no parting, no short back and sides, and rimless Glenn Miller glasses, sat before it as if he'd just taken it out of his monogrammed music-case and fitted it together. A pleasant young lady sitting in the corner, whom I'd taken to be George's girlfriend, was introduced as his sister, and a trained soprano into the bargain. With George accompanying, she recorded a couple of light operatic items, and did them very nicely. Obviously it was for this sort of thing that Mr Jackman had set up his studio. He made a good job of it. When the band struck up, though, he was out of his depth at once; he clearly could see no reason why anybody should want to preserve this kind of noise. Moreover there was the problem of balancing the sound so that the drums might at least seem not to be drowning all the other instruments. In that small room, their volume was even more terrifying.

Apart from that, the music went on to its discs quite tidily. After listening to the playbacks, George and his sister left. Had he stayed, George might have been able to put me right on a couple of things I didn't know I didn't know. The first number we did was an impromptu slow blues. I could handle that: the three chords I was getting by with were the chords of the twelve-bar blues anyway, and I think we did quite well. It was a thrill. The other tune was 'Honeysuckle Rose', which was one of the tunes I believed I knew. My job was to accompany a trumpet and a clarinet playing the tune in near-unison in the key of F. My ear had told me the first chord I needed to play wasn't F major; it must be one of the other two chords I believed existed. It isn't. But I chose one of my Flat-Earth Society chords, and banged it out for four solid bars every time it came round. It was B Flat Seventh. I also played it for the whole of the middle eight. Those who are not musicians need to be told only that these actions were very misguided indeed, and are still on my conscience, even though erased from the record, literally, by the scratching of needles, forty years since. It wasn't even an innocent ignorance: I'd got hold of the music, but had refused to believe it. G Minor Eleventh? C Thirteenth? Whose leg were they trying to pull?

My harmonies weren't the only blemish. After the opening ensemble, with its hints of Charles Ives, I had a solo piano chorus. Although continuing to use my wrong chords, I couldn't clash with anybody else, being on my own; I just seemed to be playing a different tune altogether. I also got excited, and speeded up dangerously. Then came a drum solo by the founder of the feast. It was loud, naturally. And it started at the speed I'd reached, and quickly accelerated even further. I forgot to mention that the drummer had a little red MG. The solo bore no relation to the shape of the tune; there was no way of knowing where to come in again, The closing ensemble was nasty, brutish and short. Another pound gone. And a very long three minutes.

We acknowledged the playback as pretty lifelike. It didn't occur to anybody to have a whip-round to raise a pound for another attempt. That was how we sounded, and we didn't know how to do anything about it. I couldn't afford a copy of the record; and besides, the pickup on my 1920s acoustic gramophone was so heavy that it shredded even ordinary records. I heard it only once more, about a year later. In the interim, I'd accepted conversion to the correct changes to 'Honeysuckle Rose', and was glad the record was already wearing out. The copy was the drummer's own, and he'd been listening to his solo a good deal. The blues side wasn't much worn. I wish I still had that.

I'd also, in that intervening year, tasted blood as a bandleader. I didn't taste much, and it didn't taste good. The band had decided to release me to the public as the leader of a band-within-a-band. The concept followed that of Bob Crosby's Bobcats, Woody Herman's Woodchoppers, Tommy Dorsey's Clambake Seven and the Benny Goodman Sextet: all the big bands had one. But not many four-piece bands did. The Harmonaires, or whatever the quartet called itself, was possibly unique in the audacity by which it transformed itself before the audience's very eyes, into Roy Fisher and his Students of Jazz This was done simply by removing Auntie Ivy from the piano stool and substituting me, looking suitably studious behind my glasses, and with a black bow in place of my school tie. It all happened as part of the works dance and beano of the drummer's family factory; and I was released from the protection of my family for the evening in the care of Horseface, whose craggy manner and frequent loud protestations made it clear, even to my mother, that he did not Go With Girls. So off we went from the factory gates one Autumn evening in a string of coaches to a strange pub in a spot about thirty miles away which I didn't know at all. The Nautical William was one of those Thirties Art-Deco buildings, white, with bevelled corners; it just seemed to have materialised out of the dark for one night, and, not knowing where it was, I never expected to see it again. But driving down the road from Bridgnorth to Kidderminster not long ago, I spotted it: aged a bit, but still having its own strange name, and not, so far at least, retitled 'Naughtys' – or maybe 'Willies'. Or both.

It was quite a heady evening out. My mother didn't go to works beanos, or she would have known that the scenes among which Horseface habitually passed unscathed were even more appalling than Going With Girls;

amounting at times even to what would have to be called Going With Grown Women. I'd lived with unblinking eyes through the VE Night party in our street, and I knew I could take it. There was a cabaret, with heavily painted ladies, and a blue comedian in a cream tuxedo; there was dancing, and there was drinking. Our bit, when it came, was quite painless. The Students of Jazz played their unimaginable version of 'Honeysuckle Rose' as heard on record; I played a solo version of Meade Lux Lewis's 'Bear Cat Crawl', but cut it short because I couldn't hear myself for the din of people chattering. Then the Students of Jazz reassembled for their last number ever: 'Big Noise from Winnetka', a piece popular at the time, and consisting only of a simple workout for bass, drums and whistling through the teeth. We had no bass; trumpet, clarinet and piano played the whistling bit; and the drummer went on and on, and up and up. *Kazam. Pow. Splat.* The End. He was Head of the Drawing Office as well as the boss's son; it went down very well. Somebody gave me a pound note, and I gave up bandleading.

It was the end for the Harmonaires, as well. A short while later I called on Horseface to see how things were going. He indicated, by a short expressive mime, that the drummer had found a new outlet for his hormone build-up in female form, and would never need to drum again. I don't know what form his turn at the annual works beanos took after that.

★

The deepest dive I ever played in was the Crevasse Club in Birmingham. It had a few other names in its short life, all of them to do with plumbing depths of one sort or another; but that one catches its character well enough. I didn't even know of its existence before one Monday evening in the spring of 1964, when the tenor sax player on a one-nighter in a perfectly healthy-looking, almost deserted upstairs room went broody inside his neat Italian-style dark blue suit. 'Um. Ah,' he said. 'We're starting off down the Dreaded Crevasse on Saturday. Would you care to do it?' He was a very good tenor player, decidedly ahead of my league, and the bass-player and drummer he said he'd invited were as good as anybody in town, so I was interested. 'What's it about?' I said; 'And where is it, and what time?' 'Well, it's a sort of downstairs drinking club down the back of the Fruit Market. They want us every Saturday from two till about five.' 'Two till five a.m.? What are they paying?' 'No, no, it's afternoon. I dunno about the money; but he says we can have whatever food and drink we want.'

All of that was unusual enough to get me out and into my mini-van without any lunch, the following Saturday. The instructions for finding the club had been complex, and didn't seem to help much. At that time on a Saturday the markets in the area down by Jamaica Row were winding down, and the district was a wilderness of broken cartons, dropped cauliflowers, trodden tomatoes and paper blowing about everywhere in a keen spring breeze. It was a district of big halls and warehouses, and nothing in the way of shops or restaurants; and although it was a place I knew quite well, it was almost devoid of names and signs. It didn't look promising. And it also looked deeply wrong as a place and a time for playing subterranean music.

I parked the van between heaps of vegetable refuse, and set off exploring, after locking it with particular care. Not that there was much point in locking those early minis at all. People used to lean on the door handles and pop the locks, sometimes slipping a pocket-sized length of pipe over the handles so as to increase the leverage. I comforted myself with the thought that it was broad daylight, and Digbeth Police Station was only just round the corner.

When I found the Crevasse Club, which I did a few minutes later by chasing after a double-bass which I saw disappearing up an alleyway, the thought of the police station became less reassuring. It all looked very illegal – and in a stagy sort of way, too. The alleyway, running behind a row of derelict houses, was impressively foul, with all the customary props strewn about: dustbins, chip-papers, cans, the odd car-tyre; a slow trickle of some fluid or other underfoot. The scruffy brickwork seemed to have no mortar left, but a single door in it had been painted fairly recently. It was heliotrope, but had no identifying marks. And there was no sound.

The bass-player and I stood there, looking for a knocker or a bell. There wasn't even a handle. 'Any special knock? No. Here goes.' We hammered. And again. The door swung open, and we were in, with the door shut behind us. It was a very small dark bar, completely jammed with people; underfoot there was a brick floor. 'That way down gentlemen,' said whoever had let us in. 'Your friends are waiting for you.'

With a bit of persuasion the crowd parted to let us through to the top of a flight of steps, blocked with some more crowd. Down that; and immediately down another flight, and so into a strange chamber at the bottom of it all, where the real crowd was. Not that it was waiting for us. It seemed to have plenty of amusements of its own to be getting along with. There was a piano, and a corner for us to play in, so we got ourselves together, and played a set. Everybody seemed to be happy.

Before, behind, between, above and below the customers, it was possible to work out what sort of place we were in, and what had been happening to it. We were in a small suite of dank cellars and sub-cellars and cubby-holes, the storage spaces underneath some old shop; and it had all been subjected to a right going-over. Nothing cosy or tasteful; not a whiff of flock wallpaper or Dralon. A kind of geological mutation was in progress; not finished, because in odd corners you could still see the raw edges of its creation. It was obviously done by hand. Somebody had lined the whole place with rough swags of wire-netting: pinned it to the walls, rounded out the corners, made mummy-wrappings round the brick pillars that held up the low ceilings. And a laborious crinkly coating of stiff white mush – Plaster of Paris, Polyfilla, something of that kind – had been added to the wire-netting, layer on layer, with miniature stalactites of the stuff hanging in petrified festoons overhead. Wherever you tried to move, the structure itself was crouching over you, lunging out at you, snapping off, coming off and whitening your clothes. There were a few little spotlights fixed in deep tunnels in the icing, just enough to show up the ghostly, shapeless whiteness, among which, oddly, were traces of bamboo. There was an uneven cellar floor, mostly concrete and fairly dry; and the furniture was a job lot of barrel-tables and padded casks to sit on.

As a place to play it had its points. There was no need for microphones, for the environment was of itself an amplifier; indeed, I suppose it looked rather like an enlarged version of one of those polystyrene medical models of the inside of the human ear, with curving passages and strange chambers. And surprisingly, the piano wasn't bad. But then, it hadn't been there long. Its position wasn't calculated to be good for its health; and in the three or four months of our Saturday afternoon residency it was to age rapidly. It sat on a damp concrete floor, and in the wall just behind it was the extractor fan, which sucked down to the lowest level of the establishment all the fumes of alcohol and tobacco and vented them somewhere into those streets behind the market. Before hitting the fan, those fumes were vigorously drawn, as through a filter, through the body of the piano – and of the pianist. There was a good deal of cider-drinking among the young and arty in those days, and with a sizable West Indian presence, an awful lot of 'Rumanblack' – rum, with blackcurrant cordial – went down. Even worse than all the smoke and booze vapours was the heavy, descending breath of whatever was being cooked two floors up, in what had been the old shop and was now a blacked-out coffee-bar-cum-beefburger-and-chips-dispenser. There were also various hashes, and sundry chutneys and pickles; and there was a great deal of blue smoke. I can't remember which of the club's personnel was to blame for all this. I think they took it in turns; there was certainly no chef. Whatever the source of the odours, a fair proportion of them always ended up as the same indistinguishable cocktail clogging my clothing, most of which had to go straight into the washer when I got home. And it was only on the first Saturday that I took advantage of the free food. After that I used to spend the intermissions going up for air.

In spite of the smack of illegality the club had, the police didn't raid it. I suppose they were there anyway, among the rather bohemian clientele. It was obvious that our Saturday sessions were designed to run from the time the pubs had to shut to the time they could open again at five-thirty, at which point the customers would move on to somewhere where the drinks were cheaper. While it lasted, it was a scene; it was where it was at. Most of the denizens of the city centre would turn up there sooner or later, and jabber away at one another over our noise, or that of the sitters-in, who came in increasing numbers and took over our jobs in the intervals, which got longer and longer as the weeks went by. Sometimes I'd be relieved at the keyboard by Little Stevie, who was about fourteen and shouldn't have been let in. He grew up very quickly to be Steve Winwood; he said little, and certainly didn't sing at all; but he had great stamina and many, many well-directed fingers. If he came to sit in, I'd stay and listen; otherwise it was out into the air, or up to the coffee bar where, if nobody was cooking up a whole mess of trouble on the stove, you could watch the only Scopietone in the Midlands – it was a French video jukebox, and very catchy. Pop videos still had a fresh, under-produced charm, like pre-war American soundies; and there are quite hard middle-aged men in Birmingham who can still hallucinate the Françoise Hardy item from that Scopietone.

One thing you didn't get in the Crevasse was anxious philosophising from the proprietor, a serious occupational hazard with clubs – particularly clubs which are obviously going to be short-lived. The Crevasse was owned by a pair of affable and slightly bemused brothers whose real livelihood was in some other line, like fruit machines. In the movie, the senior brother might have been played by Laird Cregar, the younger by Robert Mitchum – but that's only to say that the elder needed to wear very large spreads of dark suiting and had teeth that showed quite pearly under his little moustache, while the younger tended towards crumpled grey suits and had eyes that didn't open all the way; at least, not both at the same time. Why they owned it, I don't know. They owned it in the spirit in which people own ramshackle allotment huts or used-furniture repositories piled to the leaky ceilings with broken gas cookers and hospital bedside cabinets. Maybe they'd won it, or had it in payment for a debt. It was a club in a perpetual state of Becoming.

Indeed I once witnessed the actual process of Becoming. This was about the time I had the club positively vetted. One day in the Kardomah, my friendly Building Society Manager and Marxist Justice of the Peace laid down his Daily Telegraph and gave me a fatherly look. 'I have information' he said, 'that you are becoming involved with the activitites of the Crevasse Club. The Brothers.' 'What's the warning?' I asked. 'I don't know,' he said. 'I don't know. But, for the present – watch it. I will check it out.' The checking took a week or two. Then 'You'll be relieved to learn,' he told me, 'that according to my informants, the Crevasse Club and the Brothers are blameless. There is nothing on them.' I was surprised, rather than relieved: I should have thought the Brothers would be down for wasting police time by consistently acting in a suspicious manner, and running a deceptively disorderly house. I called in one weekday afternoon to collect some records which had been left there for me. The club was shut, but not inactive, as it turned out. I was let in by the Robert Mitchum brother, who was holding a little jamjar of something white. He led me down the stairs to where he was happily creating décor, poking wet plaster on to a new stretch of chicken wire. In the room was a young local bandleader who had just struck lucky, gone professional, and was starting to do his bit of social drinking out of hours as if his very lifestyle depended on it; and there was a table of quiet businessmen.

As I chatted to the bandleader, and the brother plastered, two young women with big shopping bags came down the stairs, in outdoor clothes. They looked like new barmaids, and we forgot they were there. A minute later there came a couple of short, disjointed blasts of Easy-Listening music; and there they were, bent over a little portable tape recorder. 'OK,' said the brother, and went on plastering his chicken-wire. The young women started the tape again, looked at each other, looked away, and took their coats off. Then, taking care not to catch anybody's eye, they took their dresses off, pretty briskly, and laid them on their shopping bags. The businessmen looked up in dismay, and pretended not to notice. 'It's just an audition,' said the brother, carefully shaping a drip into a stalactite. The girls were each already out of a layer of fancy underwear, but appeared to have several more layers to go. It was starkly embarrassing; even more so when the tape ran out before the first tune was through, and one of them tripped across, head well down, to turn it over. The bandleader and I made no excuses but left, with the businessmen not far behind. Cabaret Time at the Crevasse never really came to anything.

And the Saturday afternoon crushes came to a sudden stop quite soon. One Saturday in August I turned up to find the tenor player standing in the alley in front of the shut door. 'It's all off,' he said. 'There's been a flood. The cellar's full up. We'd be... potholing.' There was no knowing what the flood was of; I thought of the piano under a dark swirl of cider, rum-and-blackcurrant, seepage from the precarious toilets on the stairs, with sodden white plaster crumbling off to cloud the waters, and the odd swimming rat taking refuge on its lid. 'Anyway,' said the tenor player, 'they'll give me a ring when it's dried out again.'

Not unexpectedly, there was no such call. But about a year later a nice young man who owned a double-bass and was new in town rang me and asked me to do an evening session there. All was quiet; all was dry. The piano had a few stains, and it sounded a little throaty, a little distant and reproachful. Very few people in; which was as well, for the band was ragged. As for the club, it was in a kind of posthumous trance. And a few weeks later the Brothers moved to an existing but languishing club on the top floor of an office-block a couple of miles out of town. It was well above flood level, and they didn't redecorate it. Indeed, they never even opened the curtains.

*Roy Fisher*

## The Following Story

The one time I met Roy Fisher, he told me the following story. I remember it because it strikes me as a wonderful comment on his own life and work. One day in his early teens he was standing at a bus-stop with another boy I shall call Smith. Smith was 'a pompous, jolly boy', destined to be a metallurgist. Roy Fisher, who was destined to be a jazz pianist from the age of sixteen, started whistling an improvised tune, whereupon Smith stopped him, saying, 'Fisher, you can't do that.' – 'Why not?' asked Fisher. And Smith said: '*Because it doesn't exist.*'

Roy Fisher has continued getting about in his mind, composing things that didn't exist.

*Thom Gunn*

## *Left Hands and Wittgensteins*

Paul's brother Ludwig the philosopher had said
*the world is everything that is the case*
in case you lost your arm. In case you could not play
for all the world. *No left hand*
we used to say as glib precocious critics of the young
Ahmad Jamal, one of us the southpaw pitcher
on the high school baseball team who struck out every
righthand batter in the junior league.
But Paul was *all* left hand who bitched at both Ravel
and Sergei Prokofiev but nonetheless
performed their music no right hand would ever play.
The world was everything that was the case
when Blaise Cendrars also lost his arm. In that same war.
In that same war where everything that was the case
exploded in the world. My friend the southpaw pitcher studied
in the end with Leon Fleisher who awoke one day
with no right hand as a result of carpal-tunnel stress. A syn-
drome: drone, his repertory was diminished but he played
Prokofiev, he played Ravel, and all thanks due to Wittgenstein
whose world was everything that was the case.

Left hand, left wing? Roy, are all right-handers Tories
in their bones? They'd case your joint as if
they'd lost most everything left in the world.
(Or would you pack them in your case with all the world
except for B and exit in that key?) I weep
for your right arm, your stroked-out days of therapy,
your egging on your brain to find a few more millimeters
of its limb. But what's permission but commission
to a left-hand poet, left-hand pianist at seventy?
You might well go ask Wittgenstein, might well ask Cendrars.
Then go ahead – put the piano at risk, put the poem
in jeopardy: Millennium's a comin' after, Roy:
If anything could be the case
*the world is everything that is the case.*
Are those iambs, da-dah da-dah? Is that in 4/4 time?

*John Matthias*

# An Unpublished Commentary from 1966

## SOME NOTES ON *THE SHIP'S ORCHESTRA*
(Fulcrum Press, 18/-)

[I]

Art, as Imitation of Life? Or life, as imitation of art? But what of Parody? Of art as parody, even life as parody?

[II]

So what can be done with it, this business of being an artist? To bring something out of nothing? Absurd!

Or devise an arrangement that will give pleasure? But joy can't be devised or arranged. Then, as some sort of joke, laughable? And truly, desperately, nothing to be laughed at.

[III]

Why the ship? But what else could serve, what more splendid means of doing what the snail does: move and yet never leave home, never have to go away?

On the ship, within the ship, a contained place, defined, in one sense quite static and where, once set to sea, nothing can come aboard, nothing can threaten from without. As equally, of course, the joke of it: one can't leave.

And then the ocean, the movement upon it, where one mile is like the next. With water that parts in front and closes behind. No landmarks. To go forward, yet leave nothing behind.

Except of course, the wake, as evidence of transit, again like the snail.

Something fearful in this: leaving everything behind and yet nothing else behind. But also amusing. For how can one be sure that the ship really moves at all? Perhaps it has run aground and only the water flows past?

[IV]

For any artist, what must concern him most closely is the means by which he practices his art. (Note both the accuracy and irony of that: 'practices'.) Thus, for the musician, his instrument, but with a dependence and obligation in that.

For it compels work, is a taskmaster, exerts bondage, which can be shameful.

Then the only hope (since the means by which we practice can offer no escape) is to destroy that means. '...utter disposal of the instruments...' There is then another problem: if the instrument exerts the greatest tyranny, it is also the object that is most dear, perhaps the only thing that the musician really cares about.

Then the musician winces to strike, feels the pain of the blow as if against himself.

So, before the final blow, the instrument must be given protection. '...white foam-rubber containers...' These are set in further cylindrical containers. There is elaborate identification of the cylinders. Further '...a continuous white tube into which the cylinders fit and in which they are moved pneumatically...'

But no ordinary place must be imagined: 'a hanger stretching some miles in all directions...' There are further details of how it is painted, how lighted, and so on. Until the instrument itself is quite lost to view.

Thus two apparently irreconcilable and yet equally desired results are accomplished. The thing most feared and hated has become imprisoned in its wrappings, in its barracks edifice, in its prison. As the thing most loved, most precious, has been entombed and is finally safe from harm, enshrined in its temple.

[V]

'The ship's orchestra is at sea.' At sea, indeed! Then open any page at random, there is the sly: 'Inside the sack, in here with me, I think.'

To peep out, when the coast seems clear, even sneak out. 'She knows I have come out but she doesn't know where I am'.

To creep up behind her: boo! 'Between Amy's breasts by caterpillar tractor. And back again.' Teasing.

[VI]

'Suppose she wears night dresses like the heavy shining pink one always, not just when I visit. That would be no joke.' No? Then what does one mean by a joke?

Though jokes, the real ones, are not always funny. If sometimes nothing else to do but laugh. If one can, if merely the spectator.

And if one laughs, who is one laughing at, or at what? The joke on us? Which is the best joke of all and no joke.

For the orchestra does not play, or not as an orchestra. 'All the same, we're about to agree.' The members of the orchestra. 'And still the orchestra is about to agree.' Though much consideration goes into it.

And an audience? 'The question of our not being asked to play...' No longer even a question or if it was a question, what sort of question?

Though singly, to themselves they play. 'Amy has begun... Long notes, staccato notes. Methodical, clear, accurate... a killer... She must be feeling low to have to play.' To have to. The necessity, the ignominy of it.

[VII]

To date, I haven't been able to read *The Ship's Orchestra* from start to end. In fact, have difficulty reading more than two or three pages at a time. Sometimes difficulty reading more than two or three paragraphs at a time. Difficulty reading. Sense of being halted, obstructed.

Parody of *The Ship's Orchestra* even writing this. Effort to reject parody. Or not being able to reject parody. To reject obstruction. Involvement without acceptance.

Which is one aspect of its fascination, of its achievement, its achievement of a fascination. Of an inability to dispose of that fascination. Relief of anti-catharsis? Breakthrough into constriction? Assertion as contradiction?

And with the happy anticipation that I may never be able to finish it.

•

*Postscript in 1998*

This was written with the intention that it might be a 'review' of the book, although I have no memory or record of it ever being published.

However, I did send it to the author, and my excuse for finally publishing it now is that (1) it may be a curiosity, as a contemporary reaction, even a 'period' piece and (2) because I had a letter, in some extended and corroborative detail, in reply which suggested that what I wrote had not been altogether personal resonance but '...very interesting for me, too'.

Of course, whether it may still be, for that author, over thirty years later, is another matter.

*Gael Turnbull*

## *Hymn*

At the rim is all the rest
the earth can bring to burthen.
No time to be asking what
it's doing, or where

its doing's going. Sun
a gong, gone
done & swung
its darkening face across the hill

crest edge, augmented
to inaudibility. The millionth
fossilshell will go
on nursing hiss

like whatever that slick liquid is
in the comfrey bin, the distillation
out of mulch of some
thing slowly tonic.

*Tony Baker*

## Admiring Mr. Fisher's Patent Cabinet*

Opening my copy of Roy Fisher's *The Ship's Orchestra* a small piece of paper falls out. The top strip of this note has been faded by the sun to an ochre cream colour. It was probably put there in the mid 1960s when I first read this book. The note says

> p.25 Perhaps
> 26 Maybe

Turning to these page I find – 'Far off across the wet land there are conical fires *perhaps* and men turned into meat' on p.25, and on p.26 'the question of our not being asked to play has gone cold, even among ourselves. We are accepted everywhere as what we have become. People go off to bed early in the silence. The absence of music is somebody's urbane whim, and they respect it. *Maybe* there is somebody slow who will notice, tomorrow or the next day, and be indignant, just as Dougal was at first.' (my italics)

*The Ship's Orchestra*'s world is akin to Kafka's *The Castle* ('Four days at sea and they haven't asked us to play...' p.10). Also it's like one of Samuel Beckett's character's monologues with its wit and dreamlike qualities. All of which makes this such a memorable book. But it's the 'perhaps/maybe' that was so important to me (and many others?) when I first read this book, and, of course, still is. The book is full of such doubts and possibilities. ('O captain. Is it the captain? O first officer. Is it the first officer? Etc.' p.22; 'Think of Joyce's mother. An accordioniste, maybe, toothy, gilded somewhere... To turn her child into this, what can she be? Yet the girl thinks of herself as a jazz musician; talks about Blakey and Roach...' p.23)

It's the way Roy Fisher leaves areas in his 'story' open for the reader to decide, to make a choice in his or her own imagination about how it could be. It involves the reader, offers the reader numerous possibilities. Blanks or grey areas – the readers can decide and complete for themselves and in this enriching the book even more. As Borges and Fuentes recognise, each time a book is read it grows in its possibilities and 'history', expands more into the world.

Roy did the same thing, in a more muted way, in the first book I read of his, *City*, published by Migrant Press in 1961. With its very first paragraph the invitation is there. 'Occasional cars move cautiously... Their tail-lights vanish slowly into the blocks of surrounding buildings, maybe a quarter of a mile from the middle of the desolation.' I could choose, as I constructed a picture in my mind of this scene, how far I wanted the buildings to be from the 'desolation'. Just as I could decide which way the road would go up a hill in the city at night. Curving left or right over the hill? A flowing line of red tail-lights.

This quality is also there in another of Roy's earlier books, *Interiors* (Tarasque Press, 1966).

> Only a little twilight is left washing around outside, her unease interfering with it as I watch.
> Silence. Maybe some conversation. I begin:
>
> ('Experimenting')

> I cannot tell if it was he who painted the doors this colour; himself who lit the fire before I arrived.
>
> ('The Small Room')

> This seems to be the place where they wrap us in paper and tie us with string.
>
> ('The Foyer')

> You might notice my leaving. I shouldn't like that.
>
> ('The Arrival')

I could go on and on with such quotations because they are so much more striking and effective than my making some crude generalisations. They give you the feeling of Roy's work, the particulars. But it isn't just the matter of 'perhaps/maybe'. It's a far more complex bundle than that. Going hand in hand with the ideas of open possibilities for the reader is Roy's sense of 'mystery' in these works. The mysteriousness of everyday life in one's native land. I mean a very concrete form of mystery, not spooks and Magical sites, UFOs and Stonehenge built by Ancient Egyptians. I mean that genuine sense of mystery, the unknown. The startling sense of how strange and amazing or even threatening all the 'things' around us are that we take for granted. It's a sense that was so effectively explored by André Breton in his book *Nadja*. The dreamlike quality of a suburban square in Paris or, as he writes, how 'the statue of Etienne Dolet on its plinth in the Place Maubert in Paris has always fascinated me and induced unbearable discomfort…'. Roy does all this and more. But, like Breton, the 'mystery' exists in a very particular place. There's room for you and there's vivid precision and detail, and the two qualities co-exist, feed each other.

It was discovering this in Roy's work that was so exciting for me and such an encouragement when I started writing poetry, constructing poems, as opposed to earlier Dada/Beat gush. Like a sense of 'permission'? The same 'go ahead' I got from John Ashbery's poems and Jack Spicer's *Heads of the Town…* and Camus' stories and Borges' fictions. But here was Roy writing and surviving on the same island as myself, not across the oceans.

Am I labouring the point? I don't care if I am. It needs to be 'laboured'. It's still so important to stress what Roy did in these books. Something still complacently ignored by both 'Establishment' tapdancing main-chancers and 'Experimental' arrogant academics. He lets you, the reader, in. He knows you're there, not as a passive audience, but as intelligent beings and possible collaborators.

Rereading Roy's books later, with more care and attention and experience than the first time, I realised how limited my first appreciation of his work was. As well as the two qualities I'd centred on there's the amazing range and variety of Roy's writings. Also the fact that there seems to be a steady shift in Roy's work from the more dreamlike poems and prose pieces to a very concrete world, a world of history and politics. A move from the possible to the particular, though particular detail has always been the mark of his writings.

As for his range – it's almost a matter of saying open any book, take any card. In the 1971 collection *Matrix*, for example, you find three poems next to each other, each one a marvellous poem and each one dealing with a very different world. 'Continuity' with its dark city landscape where 'the exhausts patter on the dirt / stained through with oils, sterile gases.' 'Interior' and its landscape of personal tensions.

> I'm not what you want. You're not what I want. What do you do
>   with me?
> Do you take me in, with the milk in the bottom of the bottle;
>   dazzle me, with the grease spots, out of
>     reckoning?

And the long poem sequence 'Glenthorne Poems' with its vivid description of the North Somerset coast and Bristol Channel.

> No sound but breakers
> under the cliff
> the hills deep
> the sea standing
> into the cloud
> ...
> From the wrecked byre
> with dungheap
> and periwinkle bed
> two narrow fields
> fall between woods to the cliff

Roy is, as he wrote in an early poem, 'At No Distance', creating

> one various world
> beckoning infinitely
> to make me dream

to make me do;

(in *the ghost of a paper bag*)

It's a world with many locations and something always happening around the corner that we can't see but are made very much aware of. A living and shifting world. A world in depth. Right down to what's going on 'under the wallpaper'.

> There's nothing I can give you as beautiful as the flowers
>         on the wallpaper.
> Under the wallpaper, plaster, bonded with black hairs.
>         ('The Steam Crane' in *the ghost of a paper bag*)

A world where

> In a house out of sight round the shoulder,
> out of ordinary earshot,

> a desperate mother, shut in with her child,
> raves back at it when it cries,
> on and on and on, in misery and fear.
>
> ('Discovering the Form' in *Collected Poems*)

The range of 'scenes' in Roy's poetry is matched by the diversity of styles and forms he chooses. The bareness and openness of *The Cut Pages*. The relished fictions and collages in 'Hallucinations' and 'Stopped Frames and Set-Pieces'. And in contrast to this the deeply moving and direct and political (real political, small p) poem sequence, poem collage *Wonders of Obligation* (Braad Editions, 1979) and the earlier 'Handsworth Liberties' (in *The Thing about Joe Sullivan*, Carcanet, 1978). But all the pieces work, they work.

In this volume, celebrating Roy's 70th birthday it's tempting to end by quoting from his prose piece 'Releases' (*Collected Poems*).

> The greater part of my life is past, and I seem to have done nothing. Yet I've achieved rather more than I've attempted, so that means I've kept my standards.
>
> It's amazing what you can say if you try.

And that's true, but with not one jot of complacency involved. As Roy must know, Miles Davis once said – 'If you're not nervous you're not paying attention.' And Roy's nervous! as we all should hope to be. But more than this – to return to the beginning? – I think of Roy in his description of a slope of allotments in 'At Once' (in *The Thing about Joe Sullivan*): 'The stream crawls past the bottom of the slope, edged with vegetables and crossed by planks. You can approach.'

You can approach.

*Lee Harwood*   March 1999

---

★ Full specifications for the cabinet are to be found in 'Stopped Frames and Set-Pieces', included in *The Cut Pages* (Fulcrum Press, 1971), p.65.

# from *City Walking (1)*

There is a looking that is
a kind of touch,
               a fingering
beyond the body's reach.

Near Paddington,
complexity of softly
growing cloud against
a builded concrete edge.

A giant's range
but we are small enough
among the press,

walking
        reaching out.

•

Between Edgware Road
and Liverpool Street,
in a cutting:
            buddleia,
a jungle of purple flowers
sprung from London brick.

•

A wind blows under Exchange House,
below steel arch and lit offices.

It blows from an older London,
out of undercuts and passageways,
across abraded facades
and worn York paving,
through railway bridges.

It plays on
work-in-progress
on a steel skeleton,
cranes reaching high,
and, glistering,
the fuselage of a jet.

•

This place, you tell me,
is your idea of world
as it will be after you have gone.

But wind still blows round
the high buildings
of black glass and steel.

And here, tangled from his fall,
is a sculpture of one more hero
who tried to fly to heaven.

*Jeremy Hooker*

## *Multiscreen*

Waking from that dream, I find I'm in a small British provincial cinema, left over from the early 1960s. The fuzzy red seat covering irritates the backs of my legs, which seem to be wearing regulation shorts, and there's the faint smell of soap, sick and cigarette smoke. There's a documentary running which I've missed most of, and already I'm beginning to worry about my school cap. It must be a weekday afternoon showing, since so few people are here, but heaven knows what I'm doing watching it.

Grainy black-and-white. There's a lot of driving around in the desolate centre of England, in black saloons redolent of early police dramas, and a generalised hilliness: Knab Scar, Alderley Edge, Kinder Scout – that sort of thing. Bell ringers are practising inexpertly in the small villages; someone's probably about to Morris dance. No central figure has emerged, and I suppose that's important and reassuring. Cut into this there's colour footage of a tv debate going on: Professor Upright of 'one of our older Universities' is leaning back in his squishy leather chair and smiling slightly as he listens to the earnest tones of Dr. Laidback. Professor Upright is wearing a dark-but-not-sombre suit and looking distinguished, his hair greying slightly prematurely, whilst Dr. Laidback, lots of emphatic hand movement and a cheery grin, is careful to wear beaten leathers to match his stubble-and-earring. I realise with surprise that they're talking about the work of Roy Fisher, one of the country's best kept cultural secrets.

*Dr. L.:* …the urgency of the misplacing of the text, we don't need to do that in detail now, which I described more fully in my thesis. Societal factors, the more recent readings of precognitional linguistic exchange, Fisher's own strategies of self-obscuration, all lead us to place an extra value on the printed work-as-score, the vision of the 'city' as it were, which becomes, in itself, the vision of the text, undermining and destabilising our understanding of What Writing Does…

*Prof. U.:* But surely, I think you're overlooking the central Romantic Vision in Roy's work, which clearly links him to the English Landscape Tradition… whilst we all admire his fabulous sense of Irony of course, in extended works don't you feel he's really restating a Wordsworthian understanding of The Land, its History and Cultural Values. If we place these alongside comparable others, say Geoffrey Hill…

To be frank, this stuff is nothing to do with its lively and unclassifiable subject, and leaves me and others in the ragged audience a bit restless. Evidently the film crew have had enough too, for at this point they cut back to a technicolour version of the car/landscape sequence, Shining Tor, Axe Edge, Brand Side – it's all more specific now, no pussyfooting around with fancy camerawork, a country you can believe in. Behind it, I notice, there's a soundtrack, presumably it was there all the time – jazz piano with a strong striding bass and some pretty plangent attacks above it, exploring the keys, working out the relationships between them, 'experimenting' perhaps, with endless invention, deliberation and good humour. This music, it seems, has actually been directing the show for as long as I've been awake, and is far more important than the arty commentary.

I realise now that there's no earthly need for me to stay here. Stretching my stiff and prickled legs I walk out of the dingy place into the street. It's raining: the cinema is high on a hill overlooking the town in which I grew up, laid out in grim rows. If I walk hard with this beat in my head, now, into this driving rain, until my bones are cold, I'll be home.

*Richard Caddel*

## *A Dirty Poem and A Clean Poem*

> mayday 98
> Study 1
> C 20 Blues 59

1

The building was not 'backed by glowering indigo, browned
by the day and its frigid chaos', or whatever discourse
I'd once pasted it up on. Stripped out for allegory, its voiceover
prized each ethical chill. Sliding doors sluiced me
past welcome into publicity, security. Suspicion. Outside,
a police helicopter lowered in that replica New Labour Mayday sky
without cloud. We're up to *see* the Audi in the remoulded cheesegrater
as clearly as the rusted Christmas trees down the embankment!

*Be Here Now* is etched into the handless clockface
on the deserted railway platform that promises late delivery
of what could be some special trick of a lusty kitsch.
Note headless female mannikins at attention by the beds
in the department store window for the boniest of sex acts.
Fictive spans. What discourse could face this down, I ask,
facing up to what I might never simply call myself.
                                            I never
could love something without a face on it.


2

Bolting the canal's chaos beneath the night's faceless want

Haunts another category

To re-tell the job you've paid oncoming readers

Flattened out

Under the bridge a stroke as historic as now

All moons dusk the day's falling

Waste as a spectral tick in a dusty box

Create strange beings that will image

What might become stretched out almost anywhere

      *Robert Sheppard*

## Travels with Roy

There must be former students all over the country who are grateful to Roy for getting them through their degrees or convincing them that they can write poetry. In my case, what I had to thank him for is my driving licence. I arrived at Lumb Bank to be co-tutor with him on an Arvon Course when my third driving test was imminent and my confidence crushed by having failed the first two. (I was in my forties and used to being the teacher, not the dim pupil.) Roy sat calmly beside me in his nearly new Renault Fuego gazing out at the dramatic torrents of rain and sheets of lightning while I drove us around steep West Yorkshire lanes and across Widdop Moor. He knew I could drive; and back in London a few days later the examiner agreed.

I find it easier to write about Roy Fisher the human being, in the various settings, literary or otherwise, that I've shared with him over twenty years, than about Roy Fisher as poet: his reluctance to 'deviate into meaning' has gradually induced in me a parallel reluctance to deviate into critical opinions, apart from a generalised admiration. I had to do so when I reviewed his *Poems 1955-1980*, but the collection of platitudes I then came up with now embarrasses me, although I see that I quoted extracts which are still among my favourites – e.g., from 'Diversions', 'Trouble coming, on a Saturday or a Monday, / some day with a name to it: / staining the old paths trouble knows, / though I forget them.'

Back to autobiography, then: we met in Newcastle, when I was living there in 1979-81, and subsequently in a selection of places where we worked together, on courses and at festivals and readings. The most exotic was Romania, in 1984, on a British Council visit. It began disastrously when the staff at Heathrow decided to send my suitcase not to Bucharest with me but on a tour of its own, to Athens and then on a roundabout route which prevented it from catching up with me until I was back in London. Roy and I sat in the hotel foyer with Kevin McGuinness, the Cultural Attaché, discussing my plight. (Romania under Ceausescu was not a country where you could stroll into a shop and actually purchase what you needed.) Whenever Roy asked a more interesting question about the political circumstances Kevin pointed meaningfully at the ceiling: bugs. Fortunately his wife was my size and came up with a selection of basic necessities; but I was glad Roy had brought a spare toothbrush.

The unlit streets of Bucharest after dark and in a heavy shower were pretty bleak, but the Romanian writers who kept us company and told us jokes and secrets when away from offical minders animated them memorably for us. The most depressing setting in which I saw Roy was a ward in Macclesfield Hospital after his stroke – not that he himself looked depressed. I arrived feeling apprehensive about what I might find, although his letters had half reassured me. But there he was, sitting in a chair beside his bed almost like another visitor – one who merely happened never to stand up, as if, perhaps, he had a cat on his lap, or some other minor reason for staying put. His speech was unaffected, and his conversation as entertaining as ever; eventually he learned to walk again.

The regions to which we've travelled together include the past. Roy had been intermittently pursuing his ancestors for years, but had come to one of the notorious 'brick walls' beyond which no information seemed to exist. One day shortly after he'd come out of hospital our friend Joan Measham, a professional genealogist, rang me in great glee to say she'd found Roy's ancestor William Mason on the 1851 census, with his birthplace given as Avon Dassett, Warwickshire – the crucial breakthrough into a place that was not just Birmingham again. My own obsession with the detective processes of genealogy is such that I'm as happy researching someone else's as my own; and I have the advantage of access to London sources. I took over.

There followed months of chasing Masons, Pliveys, Rainbows and Paynes around a network of villages on the Warwickshire/Oxfordshire borders. At first it was in parish records and probate records, with excited phone-calls to tell Roy I'd found Richard Plivey at last, or yet another Jonas Payne. (My crowning moment occurred in Northampton Record office, where I turned up the original Jonas, granddaddy of them all, baptized at Boddington in 1628.) Then we went after them in person: Roy and Joyce booked us all into a hotel in Banbury, and we drove around the sunlit lanes to investigate churchyards. Some of the Paynes and Masons were buried at Fenny Compton, under stones shrouded in ivy; many hadn't been able to afford a stone at all. But I knew from an old list that Elizabeth Rainbow had been given one, at Burton Dassett, when she died at the age of forty in 1786. We scoured the hillside graveyard: no sign of her. It was the end of a long day, and we'd spent some time in the astonishing church, with its sloping floor and medieval carvings; Roy and Joyce were already heading for the car when I dashed back from one last look: 'I've found Elizabeth Rainbow!' There she was, under a flat stone, submerged six inches deep; someone had burrowed down into the turf and revealed a crucial patch of lettering with her name on it. Back came the others; a party of assorted children we'd met in the church joined in and scrabbled away at the soil to uncover the rest of the inscription; we all photographed it, and each other.

Such matters are not just personal; they can be the substance of poetry, as Roy's readers will understand – his work is full of places and history. I look forward to the next instalment in his transformations of experience.

*Fleur Adcock*

## *The Thing About*

When I feel down I read Roy Fisher. I think it's the meticulous minuteness of his work – say *The Ship's Orchestra* or *Ten Interiors with Various Figures* – that latches on my slowed down mind and crackles.

When I'm casting around for contrast in my reading I read Roy Fisher. I think it's the sideways perception that takes centre-stage – that gable, that piece of wall, this stretch of road – that reminds me – again – of what is important.

When I want to flee my own music I read Roy Fisher. What could be more boring than one's 'own music' and what more refreshing than *this* music. It's the thing about Roy Fisher.

Yesterday I was 'teaching' poetry again: *Experimental Anglo-Irish* poetry... It's my third year to give this particular course. Each year I try to vary it, or it varies itself somehow, in tune with the spirit of the 'experiment' I suppose. This time, weary of certainty, of 'criticism', I took in some Lego blocks and a large jar of water plus ink dropper and ink. I'm sure I needn't bother explain what I was using to explain what with. Is this a sentence?

Another year I recorded Talk One from *Talks For Words* on a cheap cassette recorder to use in a Language Skills course. That's the one that begins: 'I'm improvising this talk into a cheap cassette recorder...' I hope Roy Fisher doesn't mind. I'm improvising this on an old, borrowed typewriter.

My students, inured all their short reading lives to a simple certainty in literature, are changing their minds, I hope, a little; slowly. Roy Fisher has a lot to answer for.

'Go on.' I won't

              *Maurice Scully*

## In a Tight Corner

The social sciences library of Bradford University was, in the early 1970s, and may still be, above a skating rink. The muffled sounds of that decade's dance music would seep up to the few students at work on a Saturday morning, insidiously whispering that fun was to be had elsewhere. Though not attached to the university, I used to accompany my girlfriend there and take advantage of its contemporary poetry collection, the shelved slim volumes in mint condition. Among the many books that nobody wanted to read, I pulled out one with a sepia photograph of a pre-war street party on the jacket and decided to give it a try. I've never been able to ice skate.

In the early 1970s, the elders of Bradford, who would a few years later have David Hockney's *A Bigger Splash* banned from his home town's fleapits, were arranging for its Victorian Gothic centre (attacked by Ruskin for aesthetic-moral hypocrisy) to be replaced by a then already dated style of cheapskate brutalism. Sitting in the social sciences library, reading for the first time works such as *City*, 'For Realism' and 'The Memorial Fountain', I had in my hands a key to begin understanding the processes which were substituting one grim environment for another in the town that I would visit with my own romantic notions every other weekend. Bradford could even boast a small estate of new box-like council houses, where, in a cold December 1974, I helped deliver the Christmas post, locally called – no, not 'Toyland', but 'Toytown'.

It's been suggested recently by another poet of about my age that Fisher's writings are important because they make us 'foreign to ourselves'. That is not how it felt to read him in a half-demolished Northern town just two years after *Collected Poems 1968* had been published. I'd been introduced to a little modernist poetry ('Prufrock' and the 'Exile's Letter' from *Cathay*) in the sixth form, and followed up the lead in the school library by trying *The Waste Land* and 'Mauberley'. So even then it was possible to catch 'What are the roots that clutch, what branches grow / Out of this stony rubbish?' behind 'What steps descend, what rails conduct?' And a not-so-distant relative of the women who had asked 'What are you thinking? What thinking? What?' could be heard wondering 'At least – why can't you have more walls?' in 'Experimenting'. 'What have you been reading, then?' asks the 'I' character in the same piece: modernist poems written by men of my grandfather's generation, might have been one reply. Not only did Fisher's poetry indicate that there was a line linking me through a book published when I was sixteen to those famous works of about half a century before, it showed that such ways of writing could be directly relevant to the immediate environment. They seemed to be at work on the world where I had been born and grew.

Most of my 1970s were spent trying to teach myself how to write. The poems I published in little magazines and small press editions reveal the homage that is paid by indelible influence. Unlike the hapless student of one of the 'Paraphrases' who exclaims that 'It is / too late! for me to change / my subject to the work of a more / popular writer', I changed my doctoral dissertation topic to the work of three contemporary English poets, one of whom was the 'please Mr Fisher' of that burlesque. When I finally plucked up the courage to inform the poet of this fact (we had been in very occasional correspondence for a couple of years), he replied with a finely-wrought minimalist postcard. The printed 'University of Keele, Department of American Studies' holding-note read 'Thank you very much for your letter concerning', but had been firmly cancelled with a diagonal black line and the solitary word 'Judas!' inserted – a word whose initial shock effect was only slightly relieved by the '& best wishes, Roy'.

When crises come, they throw us back upon whatever reserves and resources we may have stored away – and so it was for me in the early years of the 1990s living in a foreign country where I couldn't speak the language, going through the accelerating break-up of that same relationship (by then a marriage) which stretched back to Bradford's social sciences library, and on top of it all undergoing major surgery for the removal of a brain tumour. The years spent compulsively reading Fisher's writings had left many echoes in the back of my head; so finally I let them act as a set of magnets for other words and phrases: 'A Well-Made Crisis', its title from the third of the 'Seven Attempted Moves', catches a moment of desolation outside the art department in Kyoto University where I was confronted by some dusty plaster casts of European sculpture; another poem, set back in England, travels down 'the old paths trouble knows' from 'Diversions'; while the sequence 'A Burning Head' recalls one more question asked in 'Experimenting' ('Perhaps you've had a child secretly sometime?') with 'You'd got pregnant once and lost it? / How come I never knew?'

The same sequence describes being allowed home to convalesce about a week after the operation:

>     Become a favourite of the night shift
>     I hardly take up any time,
>     am moved to ease bed shortages

> from ward to ward to visitors' room
> with apologies, repeated goodbyes: had left
> as if going home by gentle stages.

A glance at the earlier version of this sestet, published in *Stand*, reveals only too plainly its source: 'as if going home in easy stages' had been provided by another poem with a hospital connection. After the subsequent funeral in 'As He Came Near Death', we mourners 'got out into our coloured cars and dispersed in easy stages'. It was one of those echoes that had slipped under my guard, but the shame-faced revision is no more than a fig-leaf. 'Built for quoting in a tight-corner – / *The power of dead imaginings to return*' is how the third of the 'Diversions' describes such haunting visitations by, for example, 'the ghost of a paper bag'. In his self-review, Roy Fisher is described as 'an effective phrase-maker, and he'd be eminently quotable, if only anybody could find a reason to quote him.' But it's been among my lots in life to find a host of them.

*Peter Robinson*

## City Lights

Roy, I'm fussed by festschrifts.
Even when I promise
a piece, I either miss
the deadlines, or the lines
themselves fall dead.

I learnt from you that poems
can be lit by zinc, and smell
of currants or petrol; I
walked the wet streets
of your city memories,

hearing that childhood sneer
of the Midlands in my ear:
'You what? You must be joking.'
In Cambridge, at the Erard,
yours was a nimble answer.

Dud keys sounded for your fingers.
Let me salute you, then, as jazz man
stand up comic, fellow poet, and
for many years my bookshop companion –
filed under F – as another outsider.

*Elaine Feinstein*

*Passing Harecops*
(4 stanzas from part 5 of *Alstonefield*,
with one word specially altered)

The brightness means wholeness, the darkness
means look harder: wholeness too. Tall,
snowy beauty, year after year to look out
and see the time returned, the horse chestnut
tossing and the flakes borne up on the wind.
And in this doorway she and she returned.
And in this closure you and I survived. In
these passing violins the future of Europe
suffers a small aperture of hope, that
glows redly through the nightly smoke.

Glows pale across the fields, central affection.
Maps hoisted above the hedges, but it doesn't
matter, where to go. Don't ask, 'Where am I going?'
Ask, 'Where does such tenderness come from?'
– right there within the arms' arc, a point
that generated a history, a nothing that ran
right round the clock and back to itself year
after year as the moment fruited the bees
took their reward and the daughter that bright
instant spoke out a new justice. Where is she now?

Where fear propels and forks the path, or delight
opens into space. I'm starting to fade. Joy
lies like a stone on the ground. Pick it up
'I am alone in the night, a homeless and
sleepless nun, holding the keys to the city'
and talk it onwards, wherever you are. Carry
also something for the passing stranger.
Such are the demands of equity as love slinks
across the dark hills with the rain. I am
absolutely nothing in the showered grain.

The showered grain, the shadowed gain.
Complete silence at the crossroads, the white
railings and the sombre fields between the
dozy roads. North South East and West
where's the one I like the best because best
known, and get the knowing back. I drape
myself on the railings, towards a sleeping
lamb in a wooden crate. Daughter, let me be
a shadow on your fear, a weight on your
ambition, a red glow in your hate.

*Peter Riley*

## Get Real

It is 1971, and I have recently graduated from King's College, London, with a not-too-clever degree in English. The party's over (the Sixties; college days) and real life sickeningly beckons. What am I to do with myself? I want to 'write'. Trench-coated, I commute from Golders Green (where I briefly share a flat with a science fiction writer) to the City of London: an inconceivably dreary temp job endlessly checking invoice totals for an oil distribution company. Through a mutual mate, I hear Robert Hampson and Peter Barry, two former undergraduate colleagues, have started a poetry workshop. We meet in the Polar Bear pub in Soho. I am writing speculative fiction stories. Lunch hours spent wandering through City canyons. My parents, recent immigrants from Gibraltar, have moved to a rented flat in Archway, Mum taking up a teaching job, Dad, early-retired from the Gibraltar Civil Service, looking after an antique shop.

Like me, while at King's, Robert and Peter have come under the influence of Eric Mottram. I still remember hearing his booming laughter down the passage before even seeing his face. 'The linear novel is dead,' are the first words I remember him saying. And then later, 'Tom Raworth and Lee Harwood are the most interesting young poets in this country.'

Robert, Peter and I are reading Olson, Bunting and Roy Fisher. Endless discussion over cheap red wine and mince curry in a series of rented rooms. What do 'projective' and 'open' mean? We talk about putting a magazine together.

The Sixties may have come and gone, London has swung and been stilled, but there are still distinct Fifties hangovers. Even some of those who scoff at radicchio-and-sun-dried-tomato chic today might find it hard to come to terms (well, coming from the Mediterranean, I did) with a culture whose olive oil is only obtainable, in tiny bottles, at Boots The Chemist – for de-waxing one's ears.

Actually, it's still a bit like that as far as writing goes. My first exposure to poetry was reading Lorca in Spanish – not an affectation: I was brought up in a bilingual environment and had a schoolteacher who was a big Lorca fan. The other week in a Sunday paper a bunch of poets (the usual suspects), asked to identify the best poets of the millennium (!), failed to come up with a single non-English name.

The Fifties, The Movement (was any poetry group more inappropriately named?). How those to whom British, or more particularly, English literary culture seemed stultifying would have looked elsewhere – to France or Germany perhaps, but inevitably also the USA. Perhaps it was rock'n'roll or jazz or American movies that grabbed the attention first as representative of the enticing Other. In Roy Fisher's *The Ship's Orchestra*, the fictional jazz band (gender- and racially-balanced to a degree startling for the time), around which the author constructs a virtuoso, energised prose montage, exists in mid-ocean in a timeless topsy-turvy mode:

> At times the sea rises uniformly to become much of the sky, harmless, translucent, golden-grey, with the great sun billowing down under the keel and flaking off itself from ear to ear.

Everything is changed; strange with the logic of the imagination. I loved the writing. And the white English musicians feel compelled to reinvent themselves as Other, in solidarity with their companions:

> About five of us, then, and something of an assortment. The coloration problem touches Merritt and me more lightly, in that we are, fairly decidedly, Caucasian, although I can tell already that there's a need for one of us to feel Jewish at times, and we pass this rôle back and forth tacitly.

The magazine Robert, Peter and I are going to start is to be named *Alembic*. We are reading French Surrealism. And Donald Allen's *The New American Poetry*. I am trying to write poetry, and trying to import into my prose that sense of every word being charged. We are reading *City* by Roy Fisher, with its alternating prose and verse sequences, alongside Williams' *Paterson* and Olson's *Maximus* poems, but it is only now I recognise it as a very different beast. Despite drawing on acute observation of the topography of the poet's native post-war Birmingham, it is neither an Olsonian nor social-realist epic; rather, a work unprecedented in the literature of England, a portrait of a city of the imagination, almost Expressionist in its sense of estrangement.

> In the century that has passed since this city has become great, it has twice laid itself out in the shape of a wheel...

The author says, in answer to questions from Jed Rasula and Mike Erwin in 1973 (although I was not to read this until over a decade later):

> Most of the 'City' writing is meant to be about a city which has already turned into a city of the mind. Where the writing is topographical it's meant to do with the EFFECTS of topography, the creation of scenic moments, psychological environments, and it's not meant to be an historic/spatial city entailed to empirical reality.

And later:

> I've been told that I've been influenced by Americans. An enormous number of people come to mind, some American, some not. You might just as well, for me, talk about Rilke's Paris or Kafka's Prague or the imaginary towns that Paul Klee made up or Kokoschka's paintings of towns he worked in...

We are discovering small presses. It is autumn 1972. I have decided I am going to be a teacher, and have enrolled for Goldsmiths' College. I am reading a dog-eared copy of Michael Horovitz's 1969 Penguin anthology *Children of Albion*. A curious brew, this, perhaps the first and last time such a range of poetry could be brought unselfconsciously together. Here the Olsonesque English lyric of Andrew Crozier (starting from Gloucester in the West Country, rather than Gloucester, Massachussetts) rubs shoulders with the post-Beat rock lyrics of Pete Brown; Horovitz's own Blake- and Ginsberg-inspired bardic utterance keeps company with Tom Pickard's North East dialect poetry; Edwin Morgan eschews Scots dialect and rigorous formal experimentation in favour of an uncharacteristic paean to Ginsberg's June 1965 Royal Albert Hall performance ('Worldscene! Wordtime! Spacebreaker! Wildship! Starman!...'); Frances Horovitz contributes straightforward, if lower-cased, lyric poetry; the American expatriate painter and soon-to-be pioneer of performance art, Carlyle Reedy, is represented by two of her briefest fragments; while Adrian Mitchell's straight-ahead political polemic could not be further from the obliqueness of Tom Raworth's (perhaps no less political) fragmentation.

Roy Fisher is represented by poems extracted from larger sequences (such as 'The Entertainment of War' from *City* – a relatively conventional, well-wrought set-piece when wrenched from its context).

Things are brewing at the Poetry Society in Earls Court Square. I am too shy to connect with the scene there, but I'm beginning to recognise Allen Fisher and Pierre Joris, and of course Bob Cobbing. Eddie Linden buttonholing punters like a Glasgow barfly: 'D'ye wanna buy a *po'try* magazine?' *Alembic* 1 has come out: in loose-leaf plastic-bagged format. In my teaching practice, I introduce sixth-formers to some of the poems in *Children of Albion*. One student picks out 'The Entertainment of War' and asks me questions about it I can't answer. I meet up with Eric Mottram. He offers to introduce me to Roy Fisher, who's reading that evening at the Poetry Society. I ask Roy about the poem. He is charming, but can't hide his annoyance that that particular hit single has come up yet again.

A year on, and I've decided teaching is not for me. I start a new job as dogsbody for a small publisher of New Age books.

It's 1999. Eric Mottram is dead. I've written several books of poetry and one novel, all published by small presses. For my day job I'm working as a freelance journalist, and meanwhile running Reality Street Editions in Peckham Rye, London.

Oxford University Press has dropped its poetry list, I hear. My only concern: what's going to happen to the Bunting and Fisher titles?

They are picked up by another publisher, as it happens. But this is what Roy Fisher told Rasula and Erwin in 1973:

> ERWIN: So would you continue to write for yourself if there was no possibility of an audience?
> FISHER: I would, certainly. And if I become unpublishable I'd cheerfully go grass-roots and do what I'm always telling other people to do who write and say how can I get my books published by your publisher? Things like that. I tell them to go get working with the mimeo machine and give them away, and then do another and give that away. I do that. It doesn't matter to me.

This inspires me more than anything.

*Ken Edwards*

## *Seven Variations on Seven Random Glimpses at Page Seventy of* The Thing about Joe Sullivan *and* Poems 1955-1980 *plus a Personal Message*

One way or another it should be said that the soft parts or nine distinct reaches of the responsible – the night, Continuity, not looking, quite, it's a long story & odour – drives the Society.

Go, little book to the soft parts of the Society & nine distinct drives through odour-continuity looking to be said one way.

He's quite distinct. Driven. The Society reaches the Responsible. Another long story the night. Odour book. Said parts.

Part looking through continuity & the way another society is said to be nine books: soft reaching responsible.

Part of the night book & a little story about a Distinct continues to be said to be looking society in the eye. Quite.

One-way books are the night. Quite distinct another nine part ways said looking: drive, continue, little.

Or another way reaches the responsible story through continuity & not looking, one. One way or another one way or another one way or another


3/4 lb butter
8 oz brown sugar
1 lb oatmeal

- melt butter over a low heat
- stir in sugar & oatmeal
- press mixture onto 12".7" greased baking tin
- bake gas mark 3 for 1/2 hour approx till golden brown
- when cool cut to taste
- bring (some) on a journey

*Maurice Scully*

## The Poetry of Roy Fisher

A fixedness of attention and purpose, even a doggedness – a dog worrying a bone – to get at the matter, which is there, assuredly, evasive perhaps, but there. Or not there.

Fisher's is a probing, penetrative intelligence: large, unadorned, restless.

His work is often characterized as 'funny' or 'witty'. This is a skittishness, a stab at familiarity or amiability, in the face of a far larger, more difficult and unaccommodating project. The poems customarily regarded as *witty* are almost always poems of anger or disgust, and mirthless.

Fisher's tools, were he an artisan or laborer, would be a spade, a pick, an awl.

His lines move like that, especially in their beginnings, with a stabbing, prodding gesture. They often feel telegraphic, especially when he gets up a head of steam.

He is *realist* in the way Neils Bohr or Monet are realists.

His corpus involves a series of refusals: to be deflected; to adorn or poeticize, i.e. to charm; to inflate his subject matter or take up certain thematic material and invest it with those tonalities we identify with *important* or *major* poetry.

Fisher's outrage is deeply local or complexly interior.

He is an uncommonly painterly poet, but his landscapes often dematerialize into patterns of shadow or a world as if seen through a spectrograph.

Fisher is a social archaeologist who doesn't know when to relent; at which point he becomes a geologist, looking for signs deep among the formations and strata.

The later, extended meditative poems make use of abstraction as a kind of heavy digging equipment to plunge through the midden of his remembered and historical Birmingham in his hunt for mineral sources and the first shadowy outlines of culture and myth.

There is no poet alive whose work has challenged or interested me more.

*August Kleinzahler*

## Lament
from the film *The Black Path*

Lay the cold boys in the earth
At Mons and Hartlepool:
Prove to anyone who doubts
That blood and iron rule.
Let the river thickly speak
In tongues of silt and lead.
Teach us our impediment:
We cannot face the dead.
Run the waters furnace-red,
Afire all night long.
If we're to live then we've to make
An elemental song:
The object of the exercise
Is furnishing the world
With battleships, and thunderbolts
The gods would once have hurled.
Lay the cold boys in the earth
At Loos and Stockton town.
Still the blazing rivermouth
And shut the engines down.
Bells of lamentation preach
Like birds from every spire
To those whom nature could not teach
The language of its fire.
Lay the cold boys in the earth
At Passchendaele and Yarm.
Let the headstones hold them safe
From history and harm.
Twenty thousand men ablaze
Have found their lives outrun
As certainly as if you'd killed them
Singly with a gun.
When the tide is singing
At the steel doors of the bay,
Maybe you can catch its drift:

The world has gone away.
O when the tide is singing
At the steel doors of the bay,
Maybe you can catch its drift:
The world has gone away.

*Sean O'Brien*

# The Power of Magic

## 1

*12 February 1989*

What I hadn't remembered about Roy Fisher from brief earlier meetings was his humour. In fact, his talk about his poems was often very funny, as were some of the poems themselves. I stayed up talking with him until after 2 and the next morning we continued our talk as I showed him round Bradford on Avon.

One thing I noticed is that he feels his relative neglect, but deals with it humorously and ironically, so that he showed none of that rancour which often produces meanness & suspicion & self-pity in writers. He recognises the magnitude of his subject, and is therefore humble towards it. Later we talked about the people and the land – those weren't quite the words we used, but we were, in effect, talking about where and what and whom we come from, the 'subject' we are part of, and the reasons why an English poet with this sense of subject *has* now to approach it 'slant'.

We talked a lot about John Cowper Powys, too. Roy had once written to him and received an immediate, helpful reply but had felt that he must not burden him with another correspondence. Roy remarked on the irony that the kind of education that equips some critics to write with understanding of his poetry prevents them from understanding his use in *A Furnace* of the Powys material. What I particularly admire about Roy and his poetry is the way he brings an acute intelligence – with unconventional sources outside those that nourish much of our English intellectual & literary life – to bear on all that he knows in his area, which extends in *A Furnace* to 'deep' places across England.

Walking round Bradford with Roy I saw at once how much he notices. He knew the names of shrubs. I could even see him both appreciating the buildings and their configuration and adding the knowledge to what he already knew of the historical geography of the wool trade. Momentarily forgetting the poetry of brick in his work I had told him there isn't a brick to be seen in Bradford, which is built entirely of stone. He remembered, and joked about it when the only brick building we came upon was the Second World War pill-box beside the medieval bridge near Barton Farm.

*27 October 1992*

Roy and Joyce Fisher came to stay with us after his reading in college. He was, as ever, humorous and humane, a witty storyteller. But what I am also aware of now is the intensely lyrical quality of some of his poetry, which evokes the 'power of magic' he spoke of, in relation to the industrial Birmingham of his childhood, and also to the 'pagan' landscape of Staffordshire and Derbyshire. Talk about Philip Larkin's 'Englishness' wearies me; but there is that in Roy's work which, in evoking history and myth in English places, and the lives and deaths of Birmingham people, goes deeper. Indeed there's hardly anything in modern English poetry to compare with Roy's recording, in 'Wonders of Obligation', of the Birmingham mass graves during the Second World War, and little that has an equivalent magical potency to his presentation of the country of 'the green chapel' in *A Furnace*.

2

These journal entries indicate what Roy Fisher's poetry means to me. My first acquaintance with it was when a friend showed me a copy of the Migrant Press *City* in the early 60s. I didn't read the poem closely then but it became important to me for what I felt it represented: a modernist urban poetry written in England, a poetry of now, as distinct from the pastoral and urbane verse which establishment critics claimed to have succeeded, and displaced, modernism in England. It was ten years later that I really did read Roy Fisher, and then I devised a university course which focused on his work alongside *Briggflatts*, *Mercian Hymns*, and a selection from David Jones. It was then, too, that I was thinking about 'poetry of place' – less in terms of 'rootedness' and 'belonging', with their neo-Georgian inclinations, but more in relation to the strange reality of human life in place and time. One of the keys to my thinking was the observation in *City*: 'Most of it has never been seen'.

The power which I find in Roy Fisher's poetry now is the power of magic. He has a strong sense of social reality, but his poetry is quite different from the kind of social realism, mimetic and freighted with class attitudes, that deadens mainstream English poetry. Magic, in the tradition of John Cowper Powys and William Blake, is the transformative power of the imagination, which in Fisher is a modern version of the 'furnace' in which the brain of Blake's tyger was wrought. It is the poetic imagination conceived as a faculty that draws upon the forces of nature and creates its 'world', whether out of bricks or words, from ideas. Thus Fisher sees Birmingham as a product of the human mind, which shapes and dissolves material structures, and sees his own imagination as in part a product of that 'world', but with a freedom drawn from nature to interpret and transform its received materials.

Like Powys he is an anarchist, in the sense that he recognises the same power to make and unmake 'reality' within every person. This is the ultimate democratic poetic, which values the uniqueness of every human being, and stands in opposition to populism and all ideas that work in terms of category and class. It is based upon the conviction that 'No system describes the world', and its iconoclasm asserts the freedom of the imagination. One manifestation of this power, in *City*, is the 'man in the police court', who 'had been discovered at midnight clinging like a tree-shrew to the bars of a glass factory-roof'. In terms of the social system the man is a thief, but in the poem he is 'the creature they had brought down in the darkness'. The poem restores to him the 'luminous nerves that made him fly up'.

In *City* imaginative and natural energy is frozen by the poet's spectatorial stance, yet such images as that of the man in the police court indicate the way of imaginative release that Fisher would find in subsequent work. Thus the man with his mysteriously potent life is akin to the old woman in *A Furnace*, 'Massive in the sunlight'. Now, in the later poem, sunlight generates Fisher's 'timeless identities', whose 'making... is a primary impulse which the cosmos itself has'. Understanding this idea of the creative 'furnace', the power in which all human beings participate, we see why the poet will not pin himself down. The 'I' in Fisher's poems is, like the man, humorous and humane, but *it is not all there is*. No wonder he should ask: 'what sort of man / comes in a message?' One answer would be: the sort of poet who writes from a naively conceived self, producing poems circumscribed by the 'I'-seeing, 'I'-feeling which dams the sources of language, and abstracts both self and the world from the creativity of nature and the human mind. But I would not want my idea of the Fisher imagination to become another system. It is the power of magic in his poems that dissolves all ideas by which one tries to categorise them.

*Jeremy Hooker*

## *Bristol Night Walk*

                It is not far –
    Given the mind's propensity to travel
And not leave the spot. Morse
    From the Cabot Tower is signaling our existence
To Mars, and though there is no one there
    To appreciate the claire de terre, the pulse
Of light at the bottom of this well,
    You face all that emptiness overhead
With eqanimity, the city spread before you –
    So much movement round fixed points,
Spire, tower and bridge. The dew
    Of this warm night will leave each statue
Drenched and shining. But not yet.
    They loom now in nocturnal gravity –
Burke advancing behind the gesture of his hand,
    And through the traffic fume the horse
Bearing royal William, stretches wide
    Nostrils that look as though they scent it.
The dew is gathering under darkness,
    Glistening in silence where the bridge
Leaps the vacancy of the abyss it spans:
    We hang here balanced between iron and stone
Under the equilibrium of such stars
    As prick the vault above us, our fragility
For the moment shielded in the palm of space.

              *Charles Tomlinson*

## Freedom Forms

For one moment around 1980 it looked as if there might be a Tribe of Roy: early John Ash and Peter Robinson seemed to point towards such a possibility. For half the next moment I felt as though I might be a member. My own creative work plunged into intense monologic ventriloquizing, culminating in a poem entitled 'The Influence of Anxiety', which repeated, as nearly as I was able, the teasingly undramatised 'head voice' and cool irony of Fisher's 1970s poems about poetry. Looking through files of old poems, I cannot now find it, vanished I hope with the anxiety it played out. Perhaps I was more akin to the hapless correspondent of Fisher's poem 'Paraphrases' than I would have admitted. Meeting Roy and organising readings for him introduced me to the charm and wit of his conversation, the rigour and justice of his never dogmatic literary judgements, but it also saved me from the fate of the research student in Fisher's poem, who thinks that he *is* Roy Fisher. Here, a quarter of a century older than myself, was a man with an evidently different sensibility and history from my own.

John Ashbery says somewhere that genuine influence doesn't show. It is not a matter of replicating stylistic traces, but a deeper and respectful appreciation of kinship and difference. There was no Tribe, only a number of fellow enthusiasts to whom this extraordinary body of work spoke, in different ways. If, as Roy said, in an interview of 1973, 'a poem has business to exist... if there's a reasonable chance that somebody may have his perceptions rearranged by having read it' then I submitted myself to continual rearrangement and similarly saw the function of the poem as a 'subversive agent'. I was powerfully indebted to, and influenced by, Roy's work, in Ashbery's sense, and I emerged a writer with my own materials, my own methods, and my own poetics. I also completed a PhD whose main focus was the poetry and poetics of Roy Fisher and Lee Harwood, and I unashamedly placed Fisher's work in the context of alternative British poetry.

What appealed in his work, after my initial flirtation with the 1970s notion of a 'poetry of place', was the combination of an objectivist precision rendering a specific place, with a late Modernist apprehension of the city as an hallucinatory experience: a dialectic of the empirical and the fictive. The words I later coaxed from Roy in the interview I conducted with him, which I have come to see as a document of my own rearranging in terms of poetics, precisely summed this up. He was 'de-Anglicizing England', he said.

Defamiliarisation was no longer a literary technique; it was in the service of a quiet revolution against English self-representation, and also, by implication, against its poetry, the dominant Movement Orthodoxy. The way Fisher moves onto a new stylistic terrain, while keeping the same focus, was also a lesson in method. Think of the variations he's played on the municipal theme of Birmingham.

But I was indebted as much to Roy's commitment to the creation of singular 'freedom forms' for the articulation of each work, as to the estrangement or his thematic variation. The processual generation of *Interiors* or *The Ship's Orchestra* by system ensured its place in the British Poetry Revival of the 1960s and 1970s, with writers such as Harwood or Raworth. Its intense formalism marks it as a precursor of the work of many of the writers of the 1980s and 1990s with whom I have kept company: Allen Fisher or Adrian Clarke, for example. Indeed, even in such a context, work such as *The Cut Pages* still seems encouragingly radical, in its curiously disconnected way. Its improvised structure, with only the physicality of the page acting as a limit to acts of composition, relying on its uncertain, diminished reference, and on the reader's productive powers to assemble its acts of creative linkage, seem as 'linguistically innovative' as anything produced much later and circumscribed by that ugly phrase.

The ease of the self-referring poems of the 1970s onwards, in which a voice without personality meditates quite personally upon its perceptions and upon language, and upon the evanescent relationship between the two, belies their difficult poetic foci. In such vociferated work, one of the most intractable problems concerns the representation of self. Roy avoids the empirical lyricism of the Movement Orthodoxy by stylistically *dis*-articulating the self, even as the work's anecdotalism has increased in recent years to resemble Roy's public speaking voice. I can safely ventriloquize Roy when he writes, 'In my poems there's seldom / any *I* or *you*' because for him the lines are ironic; whereas for me, they are less so. Where once I had imitated that voice now I listen to a way of 'making forms with remarks', without overt 'influence', without anxiety. I salute the man who hauntingly inhabits this body of major poetry.

*Robert Sheppard*

## *Do Not Be Deterred*
(A texturalist poem from
'The Old Red Sandstone')

Do not be deterred
by dread of the extravagant,
for the possibilities of existence
run so deeply
there's scarcely any concept too extraordinary

with certainly something very peculiar,
indeed anomalous,
about the jaws of the Coccosteus,
the use of which in the economy of the animal
is as yet unknown,
              despite my find
of a near perfect specimen
which I have most carefully examined

revealing a group of teeth in the molar position
acting on a similar group in the intermaxillary
plus two other opposing groups at the symphysis
set at a right angle to the former

thus uniting in the one orifice
both vertical and transverse mouth.

*Gael Turnbull*

## from *Futures*

She heard the satellite continue to deviate from its orbit. But how could this be? How could it make sense to say she heard it? Well, it left a trace, which is to say, not really an auditory or visual phenomenon at all but one she could sense as a disturbance pattern 'out there'. Translated into auditory terms, the trace was a scream, or a banshee wail, with a dying fall to it, somewhere in the stratosphere of attention; visually, it could be described as a long scribble of light searing a path through a galaxy of neurones. But these are just metaphors, description. Essentially, her body plotted the satellite's errant path as it passed overhead unseen, more than a hundred miles above the city. She awoke briefly, then, moisture on her face, bruised. That would have been in the early morning, certainly before it was light.

Strange that she could have dropped off to sleep at all, but she had done so, and it was true that a faint blueness was beginning to stamp out the trapezoidal shape of her attic bedroom window; the shape telling her no less clearly than the intuited trace of the satellite (interfered with by the warble pattern of the pigeons) that she had once again returned from zero – to what, to a waking dream she dreaded? She was still drifting in and out of a zone of terror and unreal beauty, and it was as though her consciousness oscillated in an increasingly frantic rhythm before tipping over into chaos: one moment the world was constricting her, she could touch its four cosy corners (the four corners of her room, in fact) with her bare outstretched fingers; the next she was in a huge starless void between living and dying; and this sequence repeated itself with increasing rapidity.

But soon it would be properly morning. There'd be sunshine, tinged only tinily with foreboding, and that merely the promise of autumn, or its threat. Stupid. Everything would be OK again. In the small grubby kitchen on the first floor, her two golden sisters would be sitting at the table, their body language as she entered suggesting that they'd been talking about her. No reason to suppose they didn't have her best intentions at heart. Yet she wanted to escape to the fresh air. And once she had achieved this, what would there be left for her?

•

But that's still in the future. It's the future of this moment. Which is early evening. The evening before the young woman heard the satellite fall.

On the roof warmed by the setting sun, unseasonably, she reclines, bare legs drawn up, her book propped upon them. The sounds are dying down. The school at the end of the lane is silent at this time of day, and even the rumble of traffic, muffled up here, is increasingly interrupted. Now and again, there's a phased drone as an aeroplane passes way overhead, over the city.

The house she and her two companions live in is completely isolated, even though right in the midst of the inner city.

Once, all the housing in the neighbourhood was of this type: three-storeyed, built of dirty yellow brick, no foundations, simply sitting on six foot of rubble above the lost rivers of the city, terraced in row behind row. Mean streets where children played; you see them in sepia photographs preserved in the local history library. The streets remain, in some cases only vestigially; but the children now live in the awesomely beached ocean liners of modern slab and tower block estates that rim the young woman's horizon, their security lights blazing all night, beacons against the grossly imagined unknown.

The jagged edges of the brickwork tell the story of the house's wrenching from its past. Involuntarily detached from its terrace, the last of its sort, it is flanked by nothingness. Or rather, on one side by an impromptu car-park behind chain-link fencing, used by the teachers from the grim faced school. On the other by a bit of scrubby public garden: a bench whereon frequently an elderly woman might pause to rest her shopping in its wheeled bag; a length of fecally hazardous undergrowth nuzzled by a stray dog or two. On the low brick wall marking the lane's opposite side, someone has laboriously and angrily spelled out in shaky letters of white paint THIS IS NOT A DUMP. Vain protest. Rubbish lines the pavement. The lane itself is narrow, a cul-de-sac off the rat-run, used for parking during the working week, overshadowed by three massive plane trees still weighed down with leaves that autumn is already beginning to strip off.

On the roof, the young woman sees none of this. Below her, the house itself is quiet and empty. Becoming drowsy, she lets the book slip slowly from her fingers.

*Ken Edwards*

## The Slink

I had a shock in 1995 when I opened the latest issue of *Angel Exhaust* (anticipating several kilometers of Writers' Union imperatives and New Age babble), and the first thing I saw was the opening line of Roy Fisher's poem 'The Slink' –

> Round behind Harecops and up across Archford Moor,

because Harecops is the name of a house I lived in with my family from 1974 to 1978, an isolated Georgian stone farmhouse on the ridge of land between the upper Dove and Manifold valleys in north Staffordshire, a few miles from where Roy now lives. After I'd got over the initial panic (Does this poem concern *me*? does it address or invoke or in any way hint at, myself... for I'm sure Roy knows that was my house...) and established that it was nothing to do with me, I was left with a strange double-take on the poem. Because I could see good reason why he was interested in that place, what he meant by it, but I didn't see how anyone else could.

> a slope of hedged field with a road up or down.
> Zone of a few dozen acres.

He doesn't describe, he only indicates. 'Why there?' I asked him. 'Because', he answered, 'that's where it happened.'

Archford Moor extends up the ridge watershed behind Harecops: no longer a moor but an area of tilted farmland, looking, among the moderate lushness and moderate grandeur of the limestone hills, distinctly impoverished: thin sheep pasture with tufts of couch-grass and waterlogged patches, unsheltered openness with one rather small and bare farmhouse in the middle well away from the road... and for a reason: it happens to be on a sandstone inlier and so gets none of the natural drainage of limestone. Very much a back-street zone to the Peak Park attractions. That's where it happened.

What happened? The way he characterises himself, slinking round corners, lurching sideways, *behind* the town hall... A kind of instinctual socialistic demurral, a constant sideways lurch towards the 'mere ground' of humanity at large, evasion of classic rectitude in favour of bent things: jazz, the wobble of the individual soul. The first title I ever remember noticing was 'Laundromat Poems'. Bending away from the front and the centre, as by a natural gravitation to the left, like being paralysed down one side, but still pressing on until the muscular symmetry itself is pulled awry...

>       Having the
> discomfort, day and night, of a thread of language
> passing through

Not then *seeking*, not some purposeful or preferential thing, but literally an inclination, which can't be resisted: the places find him, with their visions of extent beyond neutral conformity.

So that knowing and not knowing, the names, become equivalent. As reader I'm in the same position in line 1, in my own backyard, as 16 lines later when we're suddenly in some completely different place

>             the isolated row
> of shops, beached tram. *Saltender*'s boarded up
> and the boards kicked in

which for some reason I think is on the east coast. But wherever it is it's again somewhere the world has turned its back on. And again we're only concerned with what happens there; how there and only there can the damage that we are redress itself.

How clearly these habits separate Roy Fisher's work from, at one extreme, the loose sentimentality of place which really, really wishes you to know these names because it cannot bear natural isolation, and, at the other, that coy autobiographical tease, so popular, which flaunts the names you can't know and taunts you with not being 'I'. Both these rationalisms are flung into nonsense against the power of helplessness, aghast even, at how these named and unnamed places jam into each other and through the person

>       with all its other, nameless places, such as the body inhabited in all its difficulty, the mind *inclining* (gently) to judge, all followed, all persisted, until that bent, that inclination, that poetry, has entirely separated itself from the merely structural forces which pull it away from its objects, and finally in its own terms walks straight.

>       *Peter Riley*

## *Dear Mr Fisher*

Your voice
began to murmur in my ear
somewhere near
Birmingham
              at the same time
as I clapped eyes
on a beautiful nun
running
along the platform
to enter
the third stanza of the train
like an image,
very pure, very original, very
sexy.

*Carol Ann Duffy*

## The Colors of the Days

*Monday* – blue-gray, with a band of pearl gray around the edges. Start work renaming the little flitches of colour on the paint chart. The air is chill, the sky blanched. The streets creak under a drift of powder snow, and the factories have locked their doors. There is traffic on the street below, but not much; mainly late 1940s sedans – beige, dull blue and lime-green – driving about slowly. What are they looking for?

*Tuesday* – green, the yellow-green of Pernod, a slight dip in the ride, a sour taste at the bottom of the glass. Susie says she's tired; she stayed out late at a publisher's party last night. Now the doorbell rings. Through the lens I can see a Korean gentleman standing there in the hallway holding a bunch of flowers and a large piece of notepaper, trying to deliver them to the wrong address, again. Afternoon – the month's supply of newspapers arrive from Australia. I note that the art reviewer of the Wagga Wagga *Advertiser* has attacked Monet again, to little effect.

*Wednesday* – a picnic rug, mainly light yellow, some gray along the sides, a kind of check pattern. The climate seems to be warming up. There's a dust cloud on the horizon, to the west. It can't be the Cavalry. Everyone's moving out of town, that's what it is, motors straining under the load, trailers full of junk.

*Thursday* – brown, grainy, the tint not full enough, a strip of silver trim. I decide to sit in the old leather armchair for a while. I light my pipe and read *Popular Mechanics* again, the issue that tells you how to build your own glider from balsa wood and doped khaki cloth. Dope – a kind of glue. But how do you launch it? And where would you go in the thing? I can see myself gliding high in the clear skies over Colorado looking for a suitable spot to land, a clearing beside a tumbling spring where I will build a makeshift hut and set to work carving out a niche for myself in the ravishing wilderness. Years later a prospecting party will stumble upon my high-tech ranch built into the side of a hill, the Armorglass® walls, the highball cabinet with concealed lighting, the surveillance cameras, the secret launch pad tunnel.

*Friday* – black, a stripe of white and light tan where it dips at the bottom, as the metal swoops down and then up into the evening. A knot of people are standing around on the worn green linoleum in the hallway, drinking cheap red wine from paper cups and arguing about the place of socialism in a shopping-mall culture. There's a sense of something about to happen, but not quite yet.

*Saturday* – fields of white cloth loose in the breeze, some seagulls high up, far out across the pale green water, then some yachts moving away. Susie has placed an old towel on the garden path and she's lying there, a 'Saint' detective paperback shading her face, trying to develop a tan the way you might try to develop a photograph. On that front, nothing much is happening. She's saving up to go to London, by boat. What sort of a future does she think she'll have there?
... [ *Years pass* ] ...
She comes back from Europe, old, tired and unwell, distressed at having wasted the best part of her life.

*Sunday* – a flush of red, old maroon paint with a stripe of cream shining along the flank, now the newspapers are folded, now the evening closes in with distant sounds of cool jazz leaking from a club where no one is listening – one last glass of sparkling water – and the doors bang shut with a gust of wind and rubbish in the back alley.

*John Tranter*

## Playing Dead
'He paints words with the past'

They're exhaust-caked privet colours,
lupin heads and brick dust
tracked through the glazes that time
formicas on a feel for things
like cough drops, bubble gum,
black liquorice, things with the taste
of four farthings about them,
things which aren't likely to last –
but then do, the pink or the grey
I'd just go on chewing, though
losing so quickly its flavours
through a bright, cold winter day –
mum's plum jam on an aspirin
or dandelion and burdock, bringing
back, red-flecked, the yellow
and blue of an old black eye:
'Well now, who's this in the wars?'

There were corrugated iron roofs,
daubed fences frayed with rust,
a purple forehead, badly bruised
walking right into a lamp post.
I lay pretending to be dead
under the vapour trails' white
in an ominous or mackerel sky –
but no Red Indian found me,
so I got up and walked away.
Years passed, became the compost
of time's intentness rotted down
with whatever it was I used
to slip between pedestrian fears
of policemen and dark alleys,
railway lines, the waste ground,
talking to strangers, school bullies –
whatever I use to get back home.

*Peter Robinson*

## *The Sky's Events*

Making a tour of horizons,
the early retirer opts for
ratchet-tooth outcrops, bald stones,
for whatever wilderness looks inviting,
just as the duellist will have done
– these things to stand or fall by
among tinkers, moonlighters, odd job men.

Always the eventful sky
had somewhere to get to, to come from;
storm moments, packed stresses, a theme
to hum in a grief-strewn tight corner,
the sky still brings in its revenges;
half-open, half-closed, with cloud squadrons
amassed and moving westward,
it plays up lit forms to enshroud them –
like whistling the scenery, in a word.

Far from forsaken factory,
car boot sale, and stock market quote,
the early retirer marks what he can –
making the best of each new confusion
in a dialogue with the climate.

*Peter Robinson*

## 'Come to Think of It, the Imagination': Roy Fisher in Conversation with John Kerrigan

John Kerrigan: *I'd like to start with a topic which you've discussed more than once with interviewers, but which is so important to your work that it's worth returning to every few years. You told Jed Rasula and Mike Erwin, in 1973, that, where the urban writing of* City *(1961) 'is topographical it's meant to do with the EFFECTS of topography, the creation of scenic moments, psychological environments, and it's not meant to be an historical/spatial city entailed to empirical reality'.[1] Interviewed by Robert Sheppard in 1982, you were still more dismissive of loco-descriptiveness.[2] On the evidence of 'The Burning Graves at Netherton' (1981), however, and parts of* Birmingham River *(1994), you have become more at ease with a 'poetry of place' which admits descriptive elements and even* paysage moralisé.

Roy Fisher: A short answer is that the landscape has come, with the passage of time and changes in my understanding, to moralise itself under my eye, without any nudging from me. I read it as a record of conduct as well as something subjectively transfigured.

Forty years ago when I was experiencing the materials of *City*, the Birmingham I collected was virtually synchronous. At its extremes it had no more duration than my father's lifetime: in 1959 he was dying there, at 70. And although it was starting to crumble into demolition and renewal there hung over it a sort of Faulknerian stasis – it was easy for me to lay the atmosphere (though not the plot) of *Light in August* across it. It was still very much what it had been when my father was a boy: the old hierarchical industrial buildup had been halted in the moment of rapid modernisation by the war. It was that twenty-year delay that created the *post-bellum* stasis; which in its turn made a medium in which my quite intense affective fantasy reading of the city as a stage for one character could grow. For me there was in those days no other reading to be had, or suspected.

I knew at that time that I couldn't go so far as to assume any common ground with anybody else for the way I saw things, though I might, with luck, chance upon it. So I wrote accordingly. Later I travelled more and acquired a little history – particularly after the General Election of 1979 drove my mind to take refuge in Imperial Rome in search of a moral survival kit. It's still there. Nowadays I'll name a name if the place it belongs to sits steady in my mind and doesn't wobble. But I still wouldn't want to elaborate, even to the extent of Geoffrey Grigson's short travel pieces, which I greatly admire.

*To what extent do you (even sub-consciously) think of the physicality of the poem as text as correlating with the materiality of place. Environmentalists occasionally speak of the grammar of streets, the 'textual' layout of a city, and, of course, the urban scene is full of structures which have signifying aspects. How far does this make place ripe for printing out as a poem? Given your emphasis on indeterminacy, both in the poetry and in talking about it, I can imagine that you would recoil from this sort of idea, and I seem to remember you being uncomplimentary somewhere about the maps associated with Olson, perhaps out of the same scepticism about a mimetic poem/place game. (Are poems never like maps?) But there are elements in* City, *for example, of bird's-eye place-inscription.*

I'm not snooty about Olson's own use of maps and so on (not that they're 'real') for they suited his nature perfectly. I mapped Birmingham very thoroughly in the *City* period, to feed the obsession; but found that it clogged my writing, which being never as diffuse as Olson's had mobility problems of its own.

Your question (though I understand it) is passing me by somewhat. I live a good deal in maps – some of my favourite reading – and I think the issue is tethered to the tendency I certainly have to think that a 2D map or a God's-eye aerial view is the 'truth'. We know better than that, but we don't always think accordingly. We know space is curved but we also know damn well that the earth is flat and the sun goes round it. For convenience I'll write a poem in simple linear form – usually: I have done spatial texts (collaborating with artists), like *Cultures*, but they've not been much seen – knowing full well that it is in any case at the mercy of the inevitably non-linear, temporally-unharnessed responses of anybody who might read it.

I have a certain blindness – arising, I suspect, from my lefthandedness – to design and layout, and do these things so badly I don't attempt them myself. If I were to engage in spatial mimetics I'd be so unappetised by the thought that this was a dance I couldn't do that I'd be unable to invent.

*The mobile centre of your poetry has shifted in the last couple of decades from Birmingham to rural Derbyshire. I wonder why there's been no move to something like nature poetry, now that you're out in the fields? When are we going to have your poems about pike and hawks roosting?*

I don't think there's all that much of a transition. I live on a picturesque lane driven down through his tenants' fields by the 16th century Duke of Rutland/Lancaster/somewhere else anyway – let's call it Normandy – to get the coal down from his pits on the moor 400 feet above. The house is on a field labelled at that time 'The King's Piece of Glutton'. Over the wall is a small herd of heifers bred from bulls imported as frozen embryos; they're isolated because of ringworm. The BSE incinerator's two villages away. The skyline up the road is being shipped off to underlie the second runway at Manchester Airport. Dow Low rears above us, and I'll take the dog for a walk along the edge of its Drop when I've finished this. I don't know if that's an answer.

As for a bestiary, it just doesn't happen, unless to express a grudge as in 'Top Down, Bottom Up'. There are many obvious poem-opportunities, of a celebratory or characterising nature, which don't seem to me obvious at all. If I try them they lie down and die under me. Ideas for poems come to me edge-on and have to be handled round till they're visible (try 'Mystery Poems'). As for the animals, I get on with them fine, but don't project, or mix identities with them. Most of my (mainly incidental) nature poetry deals with vistas. I've always tried to do skies, and there are plenty here.

*In one of your recorded readings, you invoke geography at its most literal-mystical, by alluding to ley lines ...*

It's OK. I don't have that particular anorak in my collection. I didn't know I'd mentioned the things. But I will admit to having read old Alfred Watkins with delight because of his unabashed wacky curiosity, which reminds me of Aubrey's. I never have any truck with large-scale schizocosmologies, but I think excitable morphologists can be instructive about our habits, especially if, like Watkins, they're evidently at least 143% wrong. What I like about Watkins was the fact that his material was so local and – he hoped – human. And he did look hard at things before getting them wrong. My own compulsive orthodox landscape-reading owes something to his appetite, that's all.

*Let's move on to the psychology of space. In your recent interview with Peter Robinson, you say that the tendency of readers 'to fix their own readings – to "see" patterns in a display which at first suggests none – is certainly true to my experience, just as it's familiar to perceptual psychologists.'[3] When talking to Rasula and Erwin, you don't make any such specific reference, but you are equally fluent about psychological/phenomenological matters.*

*What sorts of reading informed or intrigued you in this direction? Despite the importance (which you've spoken about elsewhere) of your early dream transcriptions, and of surrealism in* The Ship's Orchestra, *I don't think of you as strongly drawn to psychoanalysis, but I might be wrong. Was Merleau-Ponty your sort of thing in the Fifties? Gestalt psychology? Did your interest in painting encourage you to fall upon R.L. Gregory's* Eye and Brain *(1966) and the like? Or was your interest in perception, and especially the experience of space, entirely home-grown?*

I don't breathe psychoanalysis nowadays, but in the Fifties it impressed me with its air of authoritative revelation. Merleau-Ponty I hadn't read, and still haven't. I've long been familiar with Gregory, though; and Gombrich, particularly *Art and Illusion* [1960], gave me direct confirmation of my lifelong disposition – I seem to have been born swimming in Mutability, and readings in that area were home ground. I had some training in Educational psychology. Gestalt spoke instantly to my condition. My rather lack-lustre response to the structuralist onset, in the late Sixties, or whenever it hit popular Academia, is partly explained by that old, if partial, familiarity.

On space, it's worth saying that between the ages of about 12 and 29, when I had a corrective operation, I had very defective 3D vision, and probably compensated like mad.

*Your interest in spatial perception and cognition evidently went on for some time. It's there in the poetry of the 1970s and '80s, and you say in your Warwick interview with Helen Dennis (1984) that 'talking about perception ... makes it sound as though I'm conducting exercises in experimental psychology'. What kind of work in that developing field were you aware of? Does it trouble you, in retrospect, that some of your poetry could be read quite closely alongside experimental work by psychologists? Presumably it shouldn't, given that we can learn so much about, say,* King Lear, *by reading early modern psychology.*

I'd be very happy to feel that my guesses lie close to experimental work. I've certainly no mistrust of scientific method even though I can't practise it. The school I went to was an impressive forcing house for the production of academic and industrial scientists and technologists. The fast stream I was in progressively shed Art, Music, History and Geography – most of my life, come to think of it. I never found out how to hack it. I was a maladroit and frustrated mathematician, and an uncomprehending chemist. I think there were reliable production line methods in operation but they didn't work for me, even though they didn't, on the other hand, damp the spirits of my friends who went on to become Professors of Microbiology or distinguished metallurgists. No perceptual psychologists, though. What I called earlier a lifelong disposition towards, I suppose, a rationale for all sorts of subjective experience didn't, in spite of my school performance, arise from any hostility to science, even though my education had crippled me as a practitioner.

As for how I came to be in harmony with what experimental scientists were doing. I must always have been listening out for signs that would confirm an orientation which somehow had not been 'adequately' suppressed by early training in the ways of the world – its dominant languages, verbal, numerical, symbolic, for time, extension, direction, singularity and so forth: languages developed to a formidable extent in our culture. The questions children ask about such conundrums as the edges of space, or the paradoxes of perceived time persist as subjects of enquiry in some adults, from the pre-Socratics to modern scientists with sophisticated techniques. The experience of being faced with such problems is a perennial one. Your culture may snuff your candle instantly with a dogmatic myth or custom; it may leave you free to evade the dogma; it may treat your enquiry as vacuous and provide it with no form to proceed in. It's easy to place artists or unsubsidised scientists on that little map. Their situations are not all that dissimilar.

I think the signals I mentioned are never far beneath the surface of the culture. They're constantly present in subjective experience, and an everyday alerted mindset of the sort familiar to lovers, hobbyists, research students out of sight of land in their projects, will light up the evidences in the world around. I can remember, for instance, spotting something rum, a door into infinity left accidentally open, when I was taught, at eight or nine, a couple of Irish songs – Moore's 'Minstrel Boy' and 'The Harp That Once Through Tara's Halls'. These songs had no part in the history we knew, and nobody explained, in those Anglocentric days, where they fitted: somewhere, though, obviously. Thinking of them still blows a cold clear draught through my imagination – there was more than one world to know about. Later, any reading, in anthropology or linguistics, that brought out the plurality of systems had the same effect of deepening understanding by a dimension or two. It's hard to credit now, but children of my generation were still exposed to a crazily linear view of things by which the adventures of the Children of Israel led naturally and inevitably by way of the Incarnation to the blending of Saxon and Norman in the finest race and system that was ever created to rule the progressively-improved world. No anomalies were visible; World War II merely went to show. To duck out from that, even by the accidental hearing of a different drummer, was a relief.

*Two poems which might be thought about in this context, 'Without Location' and 'Simple Location', were composed within months of each other,[5] but other pieces come between. Did you intend to write a pair, or was the latter sprung by the former?*

They're not related by design. The echo in the titles is inadvertent. I couldn't recall the first till I looked it up.

*I should say parenthetically that in other interviews, and recorded readings, you also have difficulty in recalling your own poems, which books they are in, and so forth. Is this simply authorial modesty, or is there a scorched earth aspect to your forward movement as a writer? Is it necessary in some way for you — notwithstanding your tendency to draw material from old notebooks — to put completed poems behind you in order to write new ones?*

Nothing so lofty. I've grown very bad at housekeeping my work. When I had to tell somebody recently that I didn't know where in the house to look for a copy of my Collected I wasn't being coy. Unless moved to respond to a query I simply never happen to make time for the luxurious activity of re-reading my own work, much though I know I'd enjoy working over it. I don't blot it out of my mind, though I find it hard to gain access to the memory of writing it.

*In 'Without Location', I suppose you are stripping perceptual experience down to a process, tracking what it would be like without the constructions of place which help us organise such data. The second poem seems to turn this inside out and to identify the energies which arise from the fact of something being physically situated. I wonder how far the claustrophobia — or do I mean agoraphobia — of spatial confinement in 'Simple Location'...*

Both — 'simple' phobia —

*... arises from the particular 'dream' of line 12, or is it an everyday ordeal (compare the end of 'Seven Attempted Moves')? Did the poem literally start from a dream?*

Your interpretation of both poems hits the mark. 'Without Location' arose from its title, which is a phrase from, I think, some such venerable explainer as Eddington. I can't now place it. I just started wondering what such a concept was like as an affect. The dream in 'Simple Location', recalled from a spell of compelling dreams I'd had at the age of 19, interposed itself as I was writing.

*It would be easy to take 'Simple Location' reflexively, as being about its own inception (lines 1-2) and fleetingness (last lines), but that's always what tends to happen when the reader is at a loss. How do you feel about that sort of self-descriptive imputation in accounts of your poetry? Is it just the product of bad reading habits left by the New Criticism &c., or a legitimate response to the work (its multi-dimensionality not excluding a certain formalism)?*

This is a compositional problem I let myself in for by the liberties I allow myself and the reader. How to finesse my directions towards the degree, and kind, of indeterminacy I'm feeling the reader should be given is a mystery. Too much one way and it's in free fall, too much the other way and it's Escher.

*Well, that raises a complicated group of questions about reading. And the first one is: what qualities would the perfect Fisher reader possess? Would he or she be encyclopaedically informed – inward with the OED, the history of the Midlands, the sometimes obscure artworks you invoke in your poems, and so on, or do you reckon only on sensibility and intellectual speed?*

I suppose my ideal reader would be a woman who would nose around the back of the row of lockup garages to see what she could see, without making a song and dance about it. A literary education might be a drawback – though I do have to admit it might be a help if she'd spent at least some time at an Art School. No need to know any more about the state of contemporary British poetry than I do, even.

*Setting the drawbacks of education aside, how much literature would that reader have encountered, and would she best approach the poetry from your own background in modernism? This touches on technical issues, because the ability of first-generation modernists like Pound and Eliot to play against expectations (breaking the pentameter, and so on) was a resource which now seems lost to poets. Would perfect readers of A* Furnace *have the rhythms of Kipling in their heads, or those of William Carlos Williams and Beckett?*

The reader I just posited doesn't carry much of an obligation to be perfect: the main requirement is the faculty Pound described, of being able to be comfortable in the presence of a work of art. You're lucky if your literary education doesn't inject allergens which produce undue excitation when aroused. The hard reality is that, for socially-determined reasons, nobody outside a well-prepared class of readers with developed motivations (that is, poets mostly) is likely even to know my work exists, let alone be willing to read the words carefully one after another. So yes, that sort of person will probably have already taken Williams on.

You're right to say that a poet today who isn't deliberately atavistic inevitably works inside evolved modernism and is deprived of the old reactive impetus of a kick-off against dead habits. So far as the ideal provisioning of a reader goes, I'd be unhappy with the idea of a canonical progression of reading skills carrying the implication that the final focus of history would be the ability to read my work. I'd prefer anything that dispersed insularity; enough acquaintance with the poetries of all kinds of cultures to show how various the whole business is. I go on to boggy ground here: Kenneth Cox once took me to task for using 'poetry' as if it represented an essence, something spiritous and invocable, and separable from language. If I meant it then, I don't now.

*Finally, in the act of composition, do you address or provide only for yourself, or for the ideal reader, or are you sharply conscious of the audience of imperfect organisms that browse in poetry bookshops? Obviously the answer to that will vary across the kinds of poetry – your comic pieces are accessible in quite different ways from 'Simple Location'. But have there also been chronological changes? After the initial experience (which you have spoken about) of being shocked to find yourself read at all, has your notion of the reader and his or her relevant skills altered and consequently affected your work? Or has the evolution of the poetry entirely come out of you and your experiences (including, of course, the challenges thrown up by commissions and collaborations)?*

There was a very early stage when I wrote (but didn't publish) things so wordy that it was impossible to read them aloud, but since then I've not felt much change. I learnt early on that the alignment of writer-text-reader is subject to so many variables in the weights and lengths of the levers, with the joints so unstable, that there's no point in building hopes on it. What you're doing, if you retain the old-time anthropomorphic-cum-behavioural view of the uses of text which I still have, is blind fishing in the mind-sets and associational fields of unknown people. It's necessary to rely – whatever way you choose to bend it – on some idea of a consensual use of language among people you might converse with. I don't take it further than that. And even then that language-image consists in my overhearing myself: not far at all.

*Let's smooth the way for your imperfectly actual readers by looking at difficulties in some of the poems.*

> I'm fascinated by 'Matrix', and, with the help of your hints in the Eric Mottram interview (1976), I've detected ingredients from Monet, Böcklin's Die Toteninsel and Thomas Mann's Doctor Faustus.[6] But I wonder about some names and tags: 'B.D.' in the Böcklin description of section 3 (incidentally, in my reproduction of Die Toteninsel, the shrouded figure does not raise a hand, but I gather that the work exists in different versions); Reinagle in section 8 (not, I assume, the eighteenth-century composer who produced 'Mrs. Madison's minuet'); and Doctor Meinière in section. 9 (is this a reference to hearing-loss?).

The figure, in my unfreezing of Böcklin's freeze-frame, becomes a probably Lutheran pastor with the degree of Bachelor of Divinity. Philip Reinagle made the sumptuous and startling image of the Cereus in Thornton's *Temple of Flora*.[7] I don't know anything about him, but he could easily have composed a minuet while breathing in. Meinière was introduced to me by the medics who diagnosed me as having his disease in 1958, after which it lurked for some years, offering pronounced insecurity: it wasn't hearing I lost, but balance, the sensation of which the poem enacts. The eye surgery was meant to alleviate it, but didn't. It went away.

> Is there anything you'd like to say about the shape of the sequence as a whole?

Its origin was, not an ordinary dream, but one of those extraordinary experiences in which the dream process can be observed at its work while you're awake; and can to some extent be manipulated. It's presented to you as a complex toy, for a short while.

This experience felt very benign, and still does. The master-image was, for me, nowhere concrete or paraphrasable, but is best drawn for the reader in section 5: you'll see it's drawn in terms of something mobile in relation to itself, a thing of modes and movements, rather than something capable of being mapped. As I write this I'm reminded of the general field of apparitional challenge-locations – castles, islands, mazes – that occur in quest and journey myths and legends. Though the aesthetic of such things isn't touched on in the poem: indeed, a different one is offered – that is, my own array of images. Which is, of course, largely though not entirely made up of works of art of various levels of aspiration.

The poem's a strongly self-referential work of art which contains other works of art which are meant to be seen not as swag but as entities living on within it, and animated a little by being there. Paintings are mobilized and altered, not allowed to retain their fixity – my *Toteninsel* isn't quite Böcklin's, just as any two productions of *Hamlet* will differ. The same with music: Mann heard Leverkühn's music in his head and wrote its words, which in turn made me hear a music that came from them. A mobile Chinese whisper.

The presence of works of art wasn't programmatic. In the vision I 'saw' a location which, on examination, showed up a number of familiar art things and ideas, and also attracted others, which proceeded to float in and take up places. The whereabouts of the various sections isn't answerable. The whole thing takes place in what we used to call, come to think of it, the imagination. Anything you can't recognise, I made up. The said imagination, of course, is where one's ingested works of art continue their interactive lives. I harp on this because it's important that the art works aren't seen as arrested at the point of perception with the hard radiation they'd have if mounted as postmodernist icons.

On the master-image. It is island-ish, but also with something of brain-portraiture, as in the forms of brain-scan sections. Or those infinitely interpretable Rorschach inkblots that spread from the fold in the paper. Indeed the Dr. M. section is one in which the experience of the unstably-filled head becomes the entire world.

*How would you introduce 'Diversions' at a reading?*

I've merely warned listeners that the piece is a series of poems so slight as not to achieve titlehood; but there is a biographical subtext.

Diversions – divertissements – bagatelles – divertimenti – alternative routes through minor roads when the main highway's out of commission. All of these. Again, a field of options. The possible use for readers who can catch its tone would be, I suppose, that it enacts (but certainly doesn't dramatise) the common experience in which one's forward-moving sense is stopped dead by some occurrence which is Wholly Unacceptable but also irreversible, irremediable, not to be tinkered with, even. One just has to sweat it out for as long as it takes to regroup one's numbed faculties enough to get moving again. At such a time various flakes and flashes of life can appear, often quite small and fleeting signals. The ones that interest me, of course, are subjective perceptions rather than anything social or interpersonal. They're not obliged to be cheerful or reassuring: just clearly perceptible.

I did the 'Diversions' during a bleak and bloody-minded August, marooned in a holiday in North Wales, a place always good for clearing my eye and mind out. Most of the segments were observations at the time. I'll try to categorise them. Don't make anything of the distinction between observed and experienced.

1 Felt
2 Sourceless
3 Brought into service from a note of some years earlier
4 Assembled from relevant fragments, I think
5 Settled opinion
6 Observed
7 Observed
8 Experienced
9 Observed
10 Felt
11 Observed. On Snowdon
12 Brought into service from a note of 1962
13 Experienced
14 Experienced
15 Familiar experience, called in
16 Observed
17 Observed
18 Observed. Quarry Museum, Llanberis
19 Recalled. One of those Sunday supplement food pictures, shot from directly above
20 Observed/experienced, Aberdovey (as it still was)

*One italicised line in section 3 sticks in the mind:* 'The power of dead imaginings to return'. *That sounds like a preshock of the Powysian returns of* A Furnace. *Is it? And what is the overall place of 'Diversions' in your output?*

The line's quoted from myself, possibly a little earlier. I'd probably been making notes on that topic in a quite sober fashion when a bit of it verbalised itself in an alien manner, which I recognised as the grand and ominous lingo of heaving pentameters with which I'd been trying, unpublishably, to conquer the world twenty years before. It made me laugh, so I remembered it. I'm not often given an unforgettable line.

As for the place of 'Diversions': it was what I could do at the time. My remark in the *Rialto* self-review[8] about my preferred lengths has relevance, and you might like to think about its implications, which I've not myself worked out – something to do with post-Imagism, I suspect, as well as my disinclination for going through the routines of making free-standing, anthologisable poems stand up. I've used the casual string 'form' later but with weaker unifying principles, as the title of *It Follows That* suggests in part.

*I suppose the most extraordinary instance of connectedness in your work is 'The Trace'. That one needs no glosses; but I wonder about its inception and rationale.*

It was the product of considerable concentration, luck and tightrope-walker's nerve. Some god must have been guiding my hand: Mercury no doubt. Its method relates, I can see, to a technique I sometimes use to induce dreaming and hence sleep when my mind's too stuffed with small realities: I visualise anything I can, so long as it doesn't exist, then change it for another such, no matter what, as soon as it takes shape. Nothing familiar is admitted. The poem has no previously known image. Any management of the movement might as well be scored musically (or conducted) as described rationally. At 'all through the chamber' for instance, there's a passage where I must have felt it necessary to use definite articles to head off complete diffusion and give a glimmer of hope to anybody who wants orientation. And the quasi-couplets throughout meter the images out to suggest somebody's in charge of the adventure – that's for the benefit of the writer as much as the reader.

*'Releases' doesn't seem to be much discussed. How much weight would you give it as a statement of your poetics? How you is its I?*

It seems to be something undertaken to get going again after a long lay-off. The shape is an easy movement from childhood Handsworth memories to the mood of my leaving the place in 1972. I think all the materials were already-familiar images or notions, here looking for a home. The 'I' is my unexamined label for the introverted function of myself that thinks such thoughts. That is to say, I think it's me. Still do. In the remarks tending to poetics I'm allowing myself to be overheard, rather than proposing a programme. They do illustrate the way I habitually think, and there's nothing I'm moved to repudiate.

*What about 'The Red and the Black'?*

The poem addresses the grain of my sensibility or aesthetic, and its physical limits. I always assume I can handle subtleties, velleities, half-tones, but not anything brash. Had I been a painter I'd have needed slaves to mix my colours, for the sight of reds, yellows and blacks splurging aggressively from the tubes would have wrecked me for the day. Hence the title, which refers to Stendhal only in the sense that both the military and the priestly callings give me the repellent vapours.

*I could use some help with the last section ('A hill of galantine...').*

The galantine's just what it says: a magazine foodie photo, very hard-lit, which I actually cut out and framed and kept near my work-corner for years, the way people kept a skull as a *memento mori*. 'When you can write ME you can start to call yourself a writer', it said. About 1963, I think. This is how I brought on my writer's block. As the poem suggests, it was only when the printed meat faded into subtleties that I could approach it and get to work. That is, my only technique had been to wait for it to die before I did. No genuine action.

*Let's go on to* A Furnace. *In your interview with Robert Sheppard you relate the 'didactic', political element in your poetry to the views of Blake. You quote, of course, one of the proverbs of hell in* A Furnace, *and it's easy to see what is Blakean in the poem's concern to track the operations of authority in the organized chaos of liberal capitalism. What I'm wondering is how far the later prophetic books, such as* Jerusalem, *were also an inspiration, and, in consequence, how far you'd go towards Blake's mythical/religious side. He wasn't, after all, just an analyst of the workings of power.*

*Jerusalem* and the rest make a wonderful spectacle and I'm with Blake all the way. But I can make use only of such elements of that sort of sensibility as are capable of seeping through the matted filter of my, I suppose, mildly depressive and preoccupied nature and having the fascinating if constrained character of moorland bog streams. Forgive my metaphoric wriggling.

I'm quite unable to enter the religious mentality of generations whose intense heterodoxies existed within the assumption of Christianity as the inevitable system. Most if not all of the mentions of observances, cults, ancestor-worship, paganism and its gods in *A Furnace* are, pretty explicitly, insistently *reactive* rather than tentatively positive: a bellyaching against historical Christianity's major hijack operation. I've nothing against its excellent ethics, which I have no difficulty in separating from its *mythos*, which was nowhere nearly up to the job of a bid for world domination via the bent brain. A familiar attitude.

Obviously, I've no theology. I'm a non-practising pagan: animist, polytheist.

The Eleusinian mysteries would probably have suited my view of things, except that they'd never have got me in through the door and singing the hymns and all. I do have a sympathetic interest in the prudent guesses of hunter-gatherers and tribal farmers, concerned with cyclical repetition of things that work. My tone's not reductive. Once a *mythos* starts to rock the social boat, though... see my gnomic utterance near the close of *A Furnace*.

*To push beyond that a little. The poem ranges intellectually from philosophy of language to metaphysics. What is the pedigree of that scrutiny and celebration? It can't all be coming in from Powys. Did the Nietzsche bug ever bite you? Do you feel, with hindsight, that more than the prose-style of Wittgenstein's* Tractatus *(which you mentioned to Sheppard) affected you?*

Inevitably I'm going to disappoint you on all questions to do with intellectual provenance. The most acute of my schoolmasters had me down as 'a bit of a charlatan' and my subsequent tutors recognised (though I couldn't understand what they were getting at when they tried to reform me) that I've always been quick-witted at spotting ideas and their implications and applications but quite incapable, through laziness or native incapacity, of patiently filling them in by study. I've many interests, but no scholarship at all. Nietzsche, yes of course: got the T-shirt. Extremely impressive and engaging, though I wouldn't *follow* such a bruiser to the corner of the street. But yes, I suppose the power of the radical iconoclasm must have rubbed off. Wittgenstein: yes, I saw where he fitted in to my ever-moving picture of things. You'll find another instance in Ian Bell and Meriel Lland's essay on my links with William James,[9] whose outlook I'll have absorbed while a student, reading on the wing.

Early on, this magpie/monkey superficial acquisitiveness inevitably produced world-beating table-top diagrams of great complexity and total crankiness, and it was only when the ideas started to acquire a ballast of observation and experience (a substance I spent years trying to avoid) that they stopped making silly interconnections.

*You've said that the title 'Without Location' is 'a phrase from, I think, some such venerable explainer as Eddington'. In your 1977 interview with Peter Robinson you observe: 'We haven't a language for space-time. We haven't a four-dimensional language at all. I suppose a lot of what we're talking about here is my perhaps rather small but insistent attempt to assume that a four-dimensional perception is somehow necessary for us to have'.[10] You come back to this suggestively in your interview with*

*Helen Dennis, where you talk about 'the cosmology we have since Heisenberg and since Einstein but which is extremely, excruciatingly difficult to bend our language around. I'm writing at the moment a thing in which I am trying to describe the [e]ffect of the dimensions of space, time and other dimensions if you like being warped and subjectively bent, and... the language does not allow, we still haven't counters, for things like Einstein's space time'.[11]*

*Is the poem alluded to at Warwick* A Furnace?

Yes it is.

*Did the problems of dealing with curved space affect your choice of the double spiral as an emblem and composition device for the poem?*

Yes.

*Yeats, in later life, was interested in Einstein because his theories made the time-space schemes of* A Vision *seem more plausible. Not that I think of you as Yeatsian (though I suppose your double-spirals are not so unlike his gyres), but when it comes to space and time, should one be looking for a confluence in* A Furnace *between Powysian mysticism and advanced physics?*

Well, yes. I wasn't equipped to elaborate the confluence but I had a hunch they could coexist without fighting. It didn't really occur to me that they were opposed. That's a change from a memory of myself expostulating, around 1954, that if somebody would lend the old man a Pelican paperback guide to physics he wouldn't need to have such a crackpot set of fluids, essences and what not interrupting his stories.

*Was Eddington (especially on cosmology) a significant influence on your thinking? Did reading him in the Fifties set you up for life on post-Einsteinian physics, or were you turning to other sources in the Seventies and Eighties?*

My warning about intellectual debts will have prepared you for my failure to answer, though it's worse, probably, even than you feared. I'm not, like a journalist with a leak, concerned to protect my sources ('which of you idiots leaked the riddle of the universe to this poet?'); I simply can't remember forty years back. Ideas came out of the air, I reckon. From successive generations of Our Science Correspondent. Elaborate Third Programme Lectures in the days of intelligent radio. A gradual orientation; no *coups de foudre* deep in some particular book. There's also a compendious category which has to be entitled 'Talking to Eric Mottram': a constant feed for about fifteen years from 1963 or so.

But maybe I should give you an indication of some belts of enquiry which, while still vague – and nearer to art than to science or philosophy – may give you an idea of the pattern of the environment of relativism in which my wisps of cosmology could find purchase.

I had a reasonable undergraduate training in what was then still called Philology, and got the point of the mutability of language and its relation to the world, and of the need to maintain a nomadic attitude to matters of language. Not long after, I had this opened up further by reading Whorf and others.

In my early twenties I read considerably, if without direction, in psychoanalysis, and became used to the sensation of concepts in free rotation, free fall and infinite regress. This was OK so long as I unhitched, as I did, the authoritarianism.

In my late twenties I acquainted myself with the ur-texts and instances of the classic modernism now taught in postmodernist kindergartens but then still hot stuff: Klee, Kandinsky, Duchamp, Delaunay, Schwitters, Schoenberg and so on – encountering John Cage *en route*.

Later in the Sixties I kept pretty sharp company in Linguistics around Birmingham University, and was buried in that when the first wave of structuralists harried the Midlands: that's how I missed them.

After that I had to spend a dozen years teaching American fiction and had my learning channels blocked with novels, taking occasional flight into Cage once again, Buckminster Fuller, and the bibliographies in Norman O. Brown for fun.

*In his* TLS *review of* A Furnace, *Robert Sheppard objects to what he calls your touches of 'uncertain reverence'.*[12] *He isn't explicit about the mystical/visionary strain, but I think it's part of what he dislikes, and, perhaps rather oddly – though one recognises the move – he sees this cultural and metaphysical reverence as tied in to your willingness to be discursive. Preferring you to be phenomenologically mobile, he writes: 'Fisher is working to extend his range in this, his longest work in verse, only by working against the grain of his sensibility'. How would you respond to that?*

Robert's very perceptive, but he does have an agenda, whereas my agenda consists in not having one. There are stretches of my mentality where his otherwise valid writ simply doesn't run, and the air's not breathable for him – and why not? I imagine that in the *TLS* review Robert was alarmed in case I was about to commit *Ash Wednesday*. My tone of uncertain reverence is exactly as certain/uncertain, reverent/irreverent as I meant it to be. I go on at some length about my discursiveness and the causes of its late arrival in my recent interview with Peter Robinson.[13] The awkward truth is that, for me, to speak *in propria persona* and name names is more experimental than writing things like *The Cut Pages* and 'The Trace'. When I do it I don't want thereby to issue any signals about my relation to other writers, or to factions, or to changes in the history of the art – though I can't help doing so, it seems. I do know about these things, but on this matter I simply have to nail my colours to myself and put up with the discomfort.

*Well, I notice that in your* Birmingham Dialogue *with Paul Lester, published in 1986, the same year as* A Furnace, *you end on a note of self-doubt which isn't that far from Sheppard on discursiveness, though you see the possible weakness as that of going with the grain rather than against it: 'It seems to me now that in such work as I've done fairly recently – "Wonders of Obligation", written in 1979, various shorter pieces done since then, and particularly the long poem* A Furnace *– I have, for good or ill, turned the matter inside-out and have access to an "I" which I don't have to characterise or play games with; and thus to a pretty direct and discursive approach to a heterogeneous array of material which interests me and comes under my hand as I want it to; that is, it doesn't just squat across my path. I have to admit, rather uneasily, that I may just be at the mercy of my original material, and that my sense of mental liberation comes only as [a] consequence of the real dismantling of the industrial base, and a good deal of the physical presence, of the urban Midlands.'*[14]

I rather think that those sentences express separate ideas instead of the second being consequent upon the first. All that dismantling did in fact was to dissolve an obsessive theme. I don't think it has had any implications for my technique. The truth of the matter may in fact be the opposite to what I said, in that it was the pressure of the obsessive empirical material that set me the task of struggling towards discursiveness.

*Can we move into the text of* A Furnace, *or do you object to glossing the poem any further than you have in the published annotation?*

I've no objection to furnishing Readers' Notes, if only to save guesswork – or to head off those happy souls who would rather speculate than know.

*I ask because the poem first appeared with a preface (in the Oxford University Press edition), which at least some readers have found helpful; but this was removed for the reprint in the Bloodaxe* Dow Low Drop *(1996). It's true that the 10 footnotes which you published in the OUP edition are retained there, but they are removed to the end of the text — presumably so as to keep the pages clear for verse. Would you like to comment on these changes and what they say about difficulties in the poem?*

The machinery of *A Furnace* came about during publication. Oxford got me an Arts Council bursary to write it. On seeing the text they asked me to write a preface that might make it more accessible to readers, or something of that kind, as well as footnotes. I could see the need for some informative notes but wasn't quick-witted enough to stick out for their relegation to the end. In the poem I was particularly concerned, unusually for me, to impose a forward-rolling verbal movement through the whole piece, set against the inherently static collage-structure and the capricious shifts of focus back and forth through historical time. So I was wrong to allow eye-dropping invitations into the pattern.

I wasn't happy about writing a preface, for I saw the poem as a sealed system that would, I hoped, cook in its own juices for a reader; so I wrote something rather stiff. It was the discomfort that made me want to dispense with it at the reprint. I know it carries some useful information, which I should perhaps have incorporated somehow in the poem, though I still can't see how and where. If the poem's ever reprinted I shall probably append a more relaxed version of it along with the displaced footnotes.

*The 'Introit' of* A Furnace *is headed '2 November 1958', and it has obvious continuities with* City. *When you write, 'as if I was made / to be the knifeblade, the light-divider, / to my right the brilliance strikes out perpetually', for instance, your readers are going to recall, from near the end of the earlier sequence, 'I want to believe I live in a single world. That is why I am keeping my eyes at home while I can. The light keeps on separating the world like a table knife: it sweeps across what I see and suggests what I do not.' Does 'Introit' draw on notebooks from the* City *period, or does it rely on your memories of that time and place — almost in a Wordsworthian way?*

The passage you quote from *City* was written a year or more after the November 1958 experience, which at that time wasn't indeed written up, though I did make some notes on it – as an experience, without any thought of a writing – on the day. The materials stayed with me, hardly altering and often recalled, for over twenty-five years until *A Furnace* offered them a reason for being written up, as well as an idiom.

I forget whether I've described the provenance of the passage. The job I'd just taken up, after years of confinement in classrooms, let me loose on certain days to cruise unfamiliar corners of the Black Country in search of the schools where my students were working. My productivity was low. I couldn't then drive and my trancelike bus jouneys in odd directions at slack times of day often got me beatifically lost. This particular trip took me from Bilston to a place called Fighting Cocks. What interested me, as my account of it shows, was that the metaphysic which such spells of concentration, with their lurching renegotiations of the balance between self and world, familiarly generate took, for me, the form of a reordering of causality.

*Section I of the poem, 'Calling', starts with the line 'Waiting in blood. Get out of the pit.' Presumably this 'pit' relates to the Homeric 'trench' of section II, where the ghosts get blood to drink. But I've seen it interpreted, also, by Andrew Crozier, with reference to* I Ching.[15] *Do you wish to give any guidance?*

Before starting the poem I threw the *I Ching* for an idea of its density and direction, so as to have some quasi-external suggestion to bounce my own ideas against. Those words were in the hexagram I threw.

*'Calling' ends with a landscape feature in North Staffordshire, known as 'Lud's chapel', which (your note explains) may be the 'green chapel' of* Sir Gawain and the Green Knight. *The section starts, however, from another sort of church, ravaged by iconoclasts, 'beside the Dee'. If you had provided a note for that church too, what would it say?*

It's the main Powysian reference in that section, but I couldn't give a note on it without owning up to some oddities. In 1972 I called at the church in Llantysilio near Llangollen. It's a location in Powys's *Porius*, which is set around the home he had in Corwen. My visit was brief but I made what I thought was a detailed mental snapshot: no photographs, no notes. I called up the mental image over a dozen years later when writing the section. What I wrote suited my purpose. But when I stopped off again at the church after the poem was published I found the details of what I then saw considerably at variance with the sharp details of what I'd thought to be my memory. Squirming inwardly I decided to let the passage stand, as a tacit witness to my theme of Mutability, until such time as some pilgrim, along either the river or the text, should challenge me. You are that pilgrim. Thirteen years it's taken.

*Where things are (as against where authorities assert them to be) is a key issue or mystery in* A Furnace, *so I don't expect too literal a response. But in 'Calling' it would be useful to have some guidance as to the locations being explored in 'Late at night / as the house across the street / stands rigid to the wind...' and – in your return to 'Waiting in blood' – the haunting passage which runs 'The straight way forward / checks, turns back...'*

The first: moments picked off a quiet street near where I was living at Keele, a few years before the writing of the poem. The second: a vision. A complex of emotions and judgments which revealed itself in an unmistakably visual-spatial form at some point during the poem's inception. I couldn't begin to anatomise it.

*What pagan-satanic forces are afoot in 'The few moments in the year when the quadruped / rears on its hindlegs...'?*

Pagan, certainly. Demonising Satan wouldn't be part of my scheme. It's merely the observation that a horned creature such as a stag or bison, that carries almost all its weight of imposing detail at the front, has to heave it up and simply park it at the times when the action moves briefly to the back end. Head and horns, immobilised and helpless-looking, resemble the big ritual masks men make and wear on their shoulders: and you have the repeatable link – beast, man, god. You have art, too.

*Section III, 'Authorities', contains some of your most politically charged writing since 'Wonders of Obligation'. Would it detract from the sweep of that to identify 'The town gods' who figure so prominently? Are they the 'commonplace bosses' of the 'common / people', the local bigwigs with enough money to spend in bars? JPs and aldermen.*

None of these likely candidates. I may well have laid a false trail by being inexplicit. I'm referring back, without saying so, to a passage towards the end of *The Ship's Orchestra*, where the town gods appear. Indeed, that's all they do. They're in no sense demiurges with creative – or any other – power. They're creations of the place, apparitional and apparently in some sense meaningful, the way gipsy or hill-dwelling families can show up in town in strange vehicles on market days and interrupt the sight-lines without actually doing anything much. Fellini liked to indulge himself by punctuating narratives with such figures. In the *City* period I grew familiar with a number of them. Since they were, I suppose, fairly schizoid they looked more like emanations of the city buildings than did the moving crowds going about their business. Or like staring processional figures let out to hang around the streets.

*And would it be wild over-reading to see in the 'Sadist-voyeur / stalled and stricken' a version of the semi-autobiographical persona who seems so troubled in both texts of City?*

Not at all. It's me. Not in any confessional or narrative-making sense, but as a hindsight sketch of the implications of the muffled, unexpressed attitudes that made up my disposition at that time.

*Does the 'chamber' with its 'double spiral' early in 'Core' involve a particular archaic site, as well as in some sense a Birmingham warehouse? Should your readers be looking at surveys of Staffordshire archaeology? And do you have any hints about the 'polished black basalt / pyramid, household size'? Since it's flown into its place as 'fugitive / from all exegesis' I can see that you might not want to pin it down.*

The chamber is imagined, posited, if you like, by the surrounding references-from-life, and drawn by me from its indicators, rather as archaeologists project wholes from fragments. Newgrange is loosely referred to in the matter of the double spiral. You're right about the inexplicability of the Black Thing. Again, I plotted towards what it might be, 'saw' it, and described it. All sorts of half-references are in my memory. And it may have been a premonition of my meeting with the Aphrodite meteorite in Paphos years later, as described in 'The Dow Low Drop'. The stillness and disorder of the chamber owe something to the photos taken at the opening of Tutankhamen's tomb, as well as to physicists' attempts to make diagrams of sub-atomic dispositions.

The scene shifts to Coleman Hawkins in February '69 at the Opposite Lock nightclub, made over as per description from a canalside warehouse in Gas Street Basin by a former racing-driver called Martin Hone. The area's now a quite snazzy bit of Venetian Birmingham.

*At the end of section VI, where you talk about 'the bronze statue' of Poseidon. Does the definite article point to a particular (perhaps drowned) statue of the god?*

The most famous. The Poseidon (some would say Zeus) of Artemision, now in the National Museum in Athens.

*Thinking on from A Furnace, to the sorts of poetry which were being written about the North Midlands at about the same time, I wonder what you make of Peter Riley's*

*Lines on the Liver and* Alstonefield: *poems of your part of the world?*

I think very highly of *Lines*, and the succeeding Derbyshire poems follow it up well. His personalised, politicised landscape is completely recognisable as the one I live in. I think Peter's hard/soft/hard, straight/twisted/straight poetic is a valiant attempt to duck out from under the Impossible Poetics plastic sheet, and he's good enough to have something to show. *Lines* came out before I started living here and working up to *A Furnace*, and the Spitewinter prose piece was influential in giving me a single image for holding the elements of my land-maze.

*And what do you make of John Wilkinson's collection about Birmingham,* The Interior Planets?

John Wilkinson's a powerful and intent poet whose language is densely charged with energy-traces: it's rich with verbs, the sense of happenings, deeds, potentialities, necessities, results. Obviously some of the energy's generated by the effort of the poem: making sure the horse doesn't quit and start eating grass by way of doing scenes, moments or characters and suchlike portable or collectable goods. That would inevitably (I imagine) and disastrously break or coarsen the mobile line of language-creation he's after. Anything resembling conventional mimesis is of the 'now you see it—no you didn't' sort. It goes without saying that were there not a couple of local place-names in the text and had I not learned from odd extra-textual sources that Wilkinson had spent some time working in Birmingham I couldn't attribute what goes on in the book to any particular source on the map. So my reading's not much disabled by lumpen associations of my own. And as for what's recoverable, the cortex of somebody with knowledge of Birmingham will be as likely to be stimulated as that of somebody with knowledge of Detroit. For what it's worth, Wilkinson's Birmingham stay comes thirty years after the period of my own obsession with the city's intractable materiality and twenty years after I left it. But given the difference in time, my working milieu won't have been all that different from his: going from one beleaguered multi-racial school to another by day, by night playing often in community centres in the same areas or in Soho Road drinking clubs and shebeens as a token white in a West Indian band. The contrast is that I never felt like using any of that in writing. A different task, different language.

News for the Ear *is a tribute to you by poets who have learned from your work, and/ or been encouraged by your example. I wonder whether you have any reflections on the importance to your poetry – which has advanced with such striking independence – of knowing that others are active?*

I've never given this sort of thing much thought, and find it difficult now to get the idea in focus. I can't be comfortable with the idea of my work having directly influenced anybody else's. Since I propound nothing the only influence I'd be willing to have would be something abstract, such as the example of my perpetual struggle to be pragmatic. What I get from other writers is something equally nebulous but extremely valuable. That is, the sense I get from a heterogeneous crowd of people who certainly have no common programme and may well be mutually inimical, that I can – well – *write*, and well enough to entitle me to do what I decide. That's a help, in the only place I need it. I've never been sufficiently active to be worth inviting to serve in any gang; my collaborations have been loose and *ad hoc*. To writers who don't happen to give me the tacit approval I describe I'm tiresome, boring or invisible. That's fine.

*Ian Gregson has recently linked you with Edwin Morgan (as well as Christopher Middleton) and called you 'retro-modernists'.*[16] *Can you talk about your literary relationship with Morgan (to whom you dedicate an amusing poem in* Birmingham River*), and say whether you see him or yourself as 'retro-modernist'? Do you prefer John Ash's classification of you as 'a classic post-modernist'.*[17]

I didn't know Ian Gregson had given us that label, though I can see why he did, and there's good sense in it. Eddie Morgan is in method an opportunist and a mercurial. He's famously quick on his feet and doesn't mind being seen enjoying himself; but there's a dark thug in there, which will out. Even when he's being sentimental or frivolous he knows just what he's doing. I don't think he and I have ever discussed literature except to share occasional enjoyments.

It may be a futile avoidance, but I dodge any labelling that makes me a historical type, for I think that writers who incorporate that element into their own view of themselves have at least nibbled the housekeeper's mouse-poison: their eyes will gleam unhealthily and their fur rub off in unsightly patches. The title of John Ash's review of *The Thing About Joe Sullivan* was the first time I saw the term 'post-modern'. I thought he'd made it up for my benefit. I didn't find it hard to accept his use of it as a way of reading my work, but as soon as I saw the frictionless media-and-market-driven phantasm gathering pace in the world about me I took to ducking and weaving. I don't look at it much, since I no longer teach and so don't need to. For me it's a consequence of technological advance and the compulsion to find ways of breathing recycled air and reading recycled signals, sometimes within a dizzyingly small compass. I can't do that. 'Retro-modern', I suppose, can refer to a sort of nostalgia for the sunrise sensations radiated by early modernists, promulgated by their first apologists and filtered down into the mid-century as an optimist orthodoxy. Yes, it's still possible to enjoy and explore those sensations, though without coming anywhere near to swallowing the whole deal of Modernism, either as method or commodity. What I am, a-historically, is a sub-modernist.

*Another pair of poets – very different from each other as well as from you, but sharing your resistance to the Movement in the 1950s and learning a lot from American practice. Poets whose interest in experimental modernism hasn't prevented them from publishing with 'mainstream' presses. When did you first read Christopher Middleton and Charles Tomlinson, and what have you made of their development?*

I first encountered Tomlinson on the day in 1956 when Gael Turnbull showed me everybody I need to know about but hadn't heard of, from Olson and Creeley to Bunting and Ginsberg. I picked up on Middleton a little later and read him with interest through the Sixties. I've not followed that up adequately. Charles Tomlinson's excellence for me is as a celebratory poet, an uncommon role which he's always carried with fine observation. For that reason it's never occurred to me to expect him to develop, if that means changing. I suppose I find the later work tends often to be mediated through a conversational mode, which gets between me and what he's showing, so there's some loss of contact.

When I first read these two poets it was with a sense of relief that they wrote in the knowledge that what they were making was (to use the word as a crude shorthand) art, and not some behaviour-game round and about it. But I should qualify my judgments on my contemporaries by saying that I seldom speak from thorough knowledge based on comprehensive reading. With any poet I tend to size up the address to the work – where a poem's been sensed, how it's been managed – rather than the extension of that address, unless I'm clamped to it for some temporary reason. I think, say, of Robert Garioch or Tom Leonard or Robert Creeley, poets in whom that quality of address is immediately apparent. But there's little poetry in my head, which is filled instead with almost continuous music and optical polaroids. What poetry I harbour was mostly taken on in the years when I was nosing around the outside of the art and hadn't yet landed myself in the awkward preoccupations that came with my own work. I'm not happy that the faculty of acquisition and retention faded at that time, for it's a genuine loss: maybe a redundant defence against the temptation to mimic, which would have come easily to me. I merely record it. I listen to music still very actively. Poetry I check out.

*Looking beyond your 70th birthday, at your ongoing work, I wonder how you feel about the balance or interaction between avant-garde difficulty and the sorts of fluency which you show in 'Six Texts for a Film', the script for that documentary which Tom Pickard made of you,* Birmingham's What I Think With *(1991).*

'Six Texts...' are as they are because of medium-driven pragmatics, not a stylistic evolution. Had I been paid to write the film script in 1970 I'd probably have set *The Cut Pages* on one side for while and written the script in much the manner it had in 1991. There are many hidden loopings-back and catchings-up in my chronology.

I have, though, had intermittent inclinations to try to Redeem the Anecdote from the current waves of Sex, Shopping, Self-portraiture and Sanatoria verse. I've had it in mind that Brecht, MacDiarmid and Morgan (an un-English bunch, and given to Old Left leanings) could be uncommonly lucid and reasonably answerable without incurring charges of being cosy. I can be entertained and intrigued by the arcane, but am eternally suspicious of the mediations of priestcraft in all spheres. My present inclination, supposing I can ever get down to exercising it, is to be quite intricate and subterranean for a spell.

>John Kerrigan interviewed Roy Fisher by e-mail
>between 24 September 1998 and 20 February 1999.
>
>Cambridge/Earl Sterndale

## NOTES

1 'An Interview with Roy Fisher', in *Nineteen Poems and an Interview* (Pensnett, Staffs.: Grosseteste Press, 1975), 12-38, p. 12.
2 'Turning the Prism: An Interview with Roy Fisher', *Gargoyle* 24 (1984), 75-96; rpt. as a booklet by Toads Damp Press, London, 1986.
3 '"They Are All Gone Into the World": Roy Fisher in Conversation with Peter Robinson', in Tony Frazer, ed., *Roy Fisher: Interviews Through Time, and Selected Prose* (Plymouth: Shearsman, 1999), 104-128, p.110.
4 'Interview: Roy Fisher by Helen Dennis', University of Warwick, typescript, 126-140, p. 139.
5 15 June-6 July and 9-11 December 1975, according to Derek Slade, 'Roy Fisher: A Bibliography', in John Kerrigan and Peter Robinson, eds., *The Thing about Roy Fisher: Critical Studies* (Liverpool: Liverpool University Press, 2000).
6 'Conversation with Roy Fisher', *Saturday Morning* 1 (Spring, 1976), n.p.
7 Robert Thornton, *The Temple of Flora* (London, 1812).
8 'Roy Fisher Reviews Roy Fisher', *The Rialto* 35 (Autumn, 1996), 30-32, p. 31.
9 'Osmotic Investigations and Mutant Poems: An Americanist Poetic', in Kerrigan and Robinson, eds., *The Thing about Roy Fisher*, 106-127.
10 'Roy Fisher Talks to Peter Robinson', *Granta* 76 (June, 1977), 17-19, p. 18.
11 'Interview: Roy Fisher by Helen Dennis', 138.
12 'Timeless Identities', *Times Literary Supplement* 4342 (20 June, 1986), 677.; rpt in Robert Sheppard, *Far Language* (Exeter: Stride, 1999), 18-20.
13 '"They Are All Gone Into the World"', 104-106.
14 Paul Lester and Roy Fisher, *A Birmingham Dialogue* (Birmingham: Protean Pubs, 1986), 28-9.
15 'Signs of Identity: Roy Fisher's *A Furnace*', *PN Review* 83 [18:3] (January/February, 1992), 25-32, p. 28.
16 Ian Gregson, *Contemporary Poetry and Postmodernism: Dialogue and Estrangement* (London: Macmillan, 1996), 1, 127-191.
17 John Ash, 'A Classic Post-Modernist', review of *The Thing about Joe Sullivan*, *Atlantic Review* n.s. 2 (Autumn, 1979), 39-50.

# Notes on Contributors

FLEUR ADCOCK's collection of poems, from *Tigers* in 1967 to *Looking Back* in 1997 were published by Oxford University Press; she has recently moved to Bloodaxe, who are to publish a collected volume of her poetry in 2000.

TONY BAKER was born in South London in 1954. With a home still in the Derbyshire Peak District, he has lived in France since 1995 amongst the vineyards near Angers. His recent books and pamphlets include *To Whom It May Concern* (1991), *Valdeez* (1992); *Cable* (1995), *...Yellow, blue, tibia...* (1995), *As You Were* (1996), *from far away* (with Harry Gilonis, 1998) and *Binding Affinities* (1999). His work has appeared in *The New British Poetry* (Paladin, 1990) and *Other: British and Irish Poetry since 1970* (Wesleyan, 1999), and he has organized exhibitions at the Royal Festival Hall, London in 1997 and the Palais des Beaux Arts, Brussels in 1998.

RICHARD CADDEL has admired Roy Fisher's work for ages, and happily published it in a number of fugitive editions over two decades. He has edited Basil Bunting's *Complete Poems* (Bloodaxe, 1999) and co-edited (with Peter Quatermain) *Other: British and Irish Poetry since 1970* (Wesleyan, 1999). His own work includes *Sweet Cicely* (Taxus, 1983; reprinted Galloping Dog, 1988), *Uncertain Times* (Galloping Dog, 1990), *Larksong Signal* (Shearsman, 1997) and *Underwriter* (Maquette, 1998). A selection is forthcoming from Northern House in 2000. He lives in Durham.

CAROL ANN DUFFY has a four year old daughter and lives in Manchester. Recent publications include *The World's Wife* and *Meeting Midnight*. Her *Selected Poems* is published by Penguin.

KEN EDWARDS' collections of poetry include *Drumming and Poems* (1982), *Intensive Care* (1986), *Good Science* (1992) and *3,600 Weekends* (1993). His novel, *Futures*, was published in 1998 by Reality Street Editions, the press he runs in London. He has performed his work (writing and music) in London, Newcastle, Birmingham, Exeter, Dublin, Paris, New York, San Francisco and Prague.

ELAINE FEINSTEIN is a poet and novelist. In 1980 she was made a Fellow of the Royal Society of Literature. Her versions of Marina Tsvetaeva's poetry have recently been reissued with new poems and an updated introduction from Carcanet/OUP. Her last book of poems, *Daylight* (Carcanet, 1997), was a Poetry Book Society Recommendation; her newest volume, *Gold*, comes out in January 2000. She has recently published a biography of *Pushkin* (Weidenfield and Nicholson, UK; Ecco Press, USA), and edited *After Pushkin* – versions by contemporary poets – for the Folio Society. She is at present working on a biography of Ted Hughes.

ROY FISHER, the subject of this homage, was born on 11 June 1930 in Handsworth, Birmingham. He won a scholarship to the local grammar school, later securing a place at Birmingham University where he read English and first published poems in the student magazine. To earn a living and support a family, he went into teaching, first at a grammar school in Newton Abbot, Devon in the 1950s; he then returned to Birmingham and a job in a college of education. From 1963 to 1971 he was principal lecturer and head of the department of English and Drama at Bordesley College of Education in Birmingham, when he became a member of the department of American Studies at Keele University. Through these three decades he pursued a second career as a semi-professional jazz musician. He now lives in the Peak District. His early pamphlets, including *City* (1961) and *Ten Interiors with Various Figures* (1966) were first brought together in *Collected Poems 1968*; a larger gathering of books and pamphlets, such as *The Ship's Orchestra* (1966), *Matrix* (1971), some of *The Cut Pages* (1971) and *The Thing about Joe Sullivan* (1978), appeared from OUP as *Poems 1955-1980* (enlarged paperback edition, *Poems 1955-1987*). The long poem *A Furnace* also appeared from OUP in 1986, as did *Birmingham River* (1994). In 1996, Bloodaxe Books published *The Dow Low Drop: New and Selected Poems*.

THOM GUNN is seventy, and retired from teaching at Berkeley in 1999. His first book was *Fighting Terms* (1954) and his next book *Boss Cupid*, due in 2000.

LEE HARWOOD born in 1939, lives by the sea in Brighton & Hove, and is at present an unemployed Post Office clerk. Recent collections of poetry are *Morning Light* (Slow Dancer, 1998); *Etruscan Reader IV*, with Robin Blazer and Barbara Guest (1998); *In the mists: mountain poems* (Slow Dancer, 1993); *Rope Boy to the Rescue* (North and South, 1988) and *Crossing the frozen river: selected poems* (Paladin, 1988).

JEREMY HOOKER's most recent collections of poems are *Our Lady of Europe* (Enitharmon, 1997) and *Groundwork* (University of Nottingham Arts Centre Press, 1998), his second collaboration with the sculptor Lee Grandjean.

'City Walking (1)' was written following a walk in London with Grandjean. Hooker's critical writings include studies of David Jones and John Cowper Powys and *Writers in a Landscape* (University of Wales Press, 1996). He is professor in the School of English and Creative Studies at Bath Spa University College.

JOHN KERRIGAN is the author of many literary essays, and of *Revenge Tragedy: Aeschylus to Armageddon* (OUP, 1996). Among the works he has edited are Shakespeare's *Sonnets and 'A Lover's Complaint'* (Penguin, 1986) and an anthology of laments, *Motives of Woe: Shakespeare and 'Female Complaint'* (OUP, 1991). His reviews of recent poetry have appeared in *the Sunday Times, The Times Literary Supplement, Thumbscrew* and the *London Review of Books*.

RONALD KING is a visual artist and runs Circle Press. He collaborated with Roy Fisher on *Bluebeard's Castle* (1973), *Neighbours – We'll Not Part Tonight!* (1976), *Scenes from the Alphabet* (1978), *The Half-Year Letters* (1983), *The Left-Handed Punch* (1987), *Top Down Bottom Up* (1990), and *Anansi Company* (1992). He provided the artwork which was used in the cover design for this book.

AUGUST KLEINZAHLER is the author of *Green Sees Things in Waves*. A selection of earlier work entitled *Live from Hong Kong Nile Club* is due out in 2000 from both Farrar, Strauss & Giroux and Faber.

JOHN MATTHIAS teaches at the University of Notre Dame, edits the *Notre Dame Review* and has a new book of poems, *Pages*, due out this winter from Swallow. His 1987 translation of *The Battle of Kosovo* has just been reprinted. *WordPlayPlace*, a volume of essays on his work edited by Robert Archambeau, appeared from Swallow in 1998.

EDWIN MORGAN was born in Glasgow in 1920. He retired as Titular Professor of English at Glasgow University in 1980. In 1999 he was appointed Poet Laureate of Glasgow. His books include *Selected Poems* (Carcanet, 1985), *Collected Poems* (Carcanet, 1990), *Cyrano de Bergerac* (a translation into Scots of Rostand's play; Carcanet, 1996), *Collected Translations* (Carcanet, 1996), *Virtual and Other Realities* (Stakis Prize for Scottish Writer of the Year; Carcanet, 1997), *Demon* (Mariscat, 1999) and *Doctor Faustus* (a new version of Marlowe's play; Canongate, 1999).

SEAN O'BRIEN's fifth book of poems is to be published by Picador. Its predecessor, *Ghost Train* (OUP, 1995), won the Forward Prize. He is the author of *The Deregulated Muse: Essays on Contemporary British and Irish Poetry* (Bloodaxe, 1998 and editor of the anthology *The Firebox: Poetry in Britain and Ireland after 1945* (Picador, 1998). He is also an editor of *The Devil* magazine and writes for *The Sunday Times*, *The Guardian* and the *TLS*. For one semester a year he teaches writing at Sheffield Hallam University. He lives near Newcastle upon Tyne.

PETER RILEY was born in 1940 in Stockport, near Manchester. Since 1985 he has lived in Cambridge, where he operates the last surviving mail-order poetry book business. His poetry has appeared in ten principal collections: *Love-Strife Machine* (1968), *The Linear Journal* (1973), *Lines on the Liver* (1981), *Tracks and Mineshafts* (1983), *Sea Watches* (1991), *Distant Points* (1995), *Noon Province* (1996), *Alstonefield* (1995) and *Snow has Settled...Bury Me Here* (1997). A *Selected Poems* is due in the year 2000.

PETER ROBINSON's four books of poetry are *Overdrawn Account* (Many Press, 1980), *This Other Life* (Carcanet, 1988), *Entertaining Fates* (Carcanet, 1992) and *Lost and Found* (Carcanet, 1997). His translations include *Selected Poems of Vittorio Sereni* (Anvil, 1990). A volume of critical writings, *In the Circumstances: about Poems and Poets*, was published by OUP in 1992. He has co-edited with John Kerrigan *The Thing about Roy Fisher: Critical Studies* (Liverpool University Press, 2000).

MAURICE SCULLY was born in Dublin in 1952. His books include *5 Freedoms of Movement*, *Zulu Dynamite*, *The Basic Colours* and *Steps*. A new edition of *Etruscan Reader IV* features a section from *5 Freedoms* and the central section from *Adherence* (book 5 of *Livelihood*).

ROBERT SHEPPARD's volumes of poetry, from Stride, include *The Flashlight Sonata* (1993) and *Empty Diaries* (1998), both parts of a long project Twentieth Century Blues. Recently anthologised in *Other: British and Irish Poetry since 1970* (Wesleyan, 1999). *Far Language* (Stride, 1999) collects shorter articles on poetry and poetics, including two of the many he has written on the work of Roy Fisher. He is Senior Lecturer in English and Writing Studies at Edge Hill College of Higher Education.

CHARLES TOMLINSON's *Selected Poems 1955-1997* appeared in 1997 from Oxford and New Directions. His most recent volume, *The Vineyard above the Sea*, was published by Carcanet.

JOHN TRANTER has published thirteen collections, including a *Selected Poems* in 1982 (Hale & Iremonger), *The Floor of Heaven*, a book-length sequence of four verse narratives, appeared from Harper Collins in 1992, *Gasoline Kisses* (Equipage, Cambridge) in 1997, *Late Night Radio* (Polygon, Edinburgh) in 1998, and *Different Hands* (Folio/Fremantle Arts Centre Press), a collection of seven experimental prose pieces, also in 1998. He is the editor of the Internet magazine *Jacket*.

GAEL TURNBULL was born in Edinburgh in 1928, where he now lives after much of a life spent in England, the United States and Canada. His most recent book is *For Whose Delight* (Mariscat). With Michael Shayer, through Migrant Press, he published the first edition of Roy Fisher's *City* in 1961.

ALSO AVAILABLE

# BINARY MYTHS 2
## correspondences with poet-editors
### edited by Andy Brown

Correspondences with Gillian Allnutt, Neil Astley, Tilla Brading, Ken Edwards, Peter Finch, Janet Fisher, Linda France, John Kinsella, Rupert Loydell, David Morley, Sean O'Brien, Maggie O'Sullivan, Don Paterson and Deryn Rees-Jones.

Given that the market is far smaller than the number of poets producing poems; that poets are generally the main readers of other poets' work; and that poetry itself is super-abundant, what are the motivations of publishing houses and poetry editors? How do they select work? What do they select? What do they choose to leave out, or leave to others, and why? Why do we need more poetry books?

From reviews of *Binary Myths*:

'There are precious few British publishers who address themselves to producing books concerned with poetics. Stride is one of them and both they and Andy Brown have come up with a stimulating book, well worth reading.'
*Poetry Quarterly Review*

'A stimulating read and brave a attempt to map out portions of contemporary poetry's chaotic landscape.'
*Orbis*

*Binary Myths 2* is available for £8.95, post free, from the publisher:
**STRIDE PUBLICATIONS**
**11 SYLVAN ROAD, EXETER, DEVON EX4 6EW**
*(cheques payable to 'Stride' please)*

ALSO AVAILABLE

# FAR LANGUAGE
poetics and linguistically innovative poetry 1978-1997
by Robert Sheppard

*Far Language* is a concise critical survey of the alternative poetries of Britain; yet it amounts to more than that. Sheppard always writes as a poet, sometimes devising forms for his perceptions, and he offers an insider's view of this poetry scene. Originally written for a variety of publications, ranging from national weeklies to poetry journals, these pieces have been selected to reflect the development of a theory of poetry. Some of them review the work of particular writers, including Roy Fisher, J.H. Prynne, Lee Harwood and Tom Raworth; and whereas many accounts of this poetry focus on these well-known names of the 1960s, this volume updates with features on Veronica Forrest-Thomson, Allen Fisher, Ulli Freer and Maggie O'Sullivan and other more recent writers.

Some pieces here speak, often polemically, of a broader poetics, and as eloquently mediate this for a school audience as articulate it in the light of the postmodern thought of Lyotard, Derrida, and Deleuze & Guattari. The pieces range from a reflection upon the work of Bob Cobbing, with its snapshots of dozens of writers associated with his radical Writers Forum press and workshops, through to an account of the personal poetics of Sheppard's creative project of recent years *Twentieth Century Blues*.

'An intelligent theorist and commentator as well as an excellent poet...'
   Ken Edwards

*Far Language* is available for £6.95, post free, from the publisher:
**STRIDE PUBLICATIONS**
**11 SYLVAN ROAD, EXETER, DEVON EX4 6EW**
*(cheques payable to 'Stride' please)*